PEACE WITH YO

Erik Blumenthal Dip. Psych. (born in 1914) is a practising psychotherapist and analyst. He is a lecturer at the Alfred Adler Institute in Zürich, President of the Swiss Society for Individual Psychology, and Director of the International Committee for Adlerian Summer Schools and Institutes. He is also a member of the Bahá'í Faith. He has written a number of books on child-rearing, self-education, marriage and old age, and is married with six children and nine grandchildren.

Books by the same author

To Understand and Be Understood
The Way to Inner Freedom

PEACE WITH YOUR PARTNER

A Practical Guide to Happy Marriage

Erik Blumenthal

ONEWORLD

PEACE WITH YOUR PARTNER

Oneworld Publications Ltd
(Sales and Editorial)
185 Banbury Road, Oxford OX2 7AR, England

Oneworld Publications Ltd
(U.S. Sales Office)
County Route 9, P.O. Box 357
Chatham, N.Y. 12037, USA

Translated by Rosy Border and Colin Brett

ISBN 1–85168–020–9

Phototypeset by Intype, London

Printed and bound by Guernsey Press

CONTENTS

FOREWORD

Why do two people choose to spend their lives together? The primary reason is a desire for unity. Two individuals make one couple – always providing that those two individuals can live together in peace, understanding and harmony. What gets in the way of this harmony? In a peace declaration issued in the UN Year of Peace, 1986, we read:

'Indeed, so much have aggression and conflict come to characterize our social, economic and religious systems, that many have succumbed to the view that such behaviour is intrinsic to human nature and therefore ineradicable. With the entrenchment of this view, a paralysing contradiction has developed in human affairs. On the one hand, people of all nations proclaim not only their readiness but their longing for peace and harmony, for an end to the harrowing apprehensions tormenting their daily lives. On the other, uncritical assent is given to the proposition that human beings are incorrigibly selfish and aggressive and thus incapable of erecting a social system at once progressive and peaceful, dynamic and harmonious,

9

a system giving free play to individual creativity and initiative but based on co-operation and reciprocity.'[1]

Modern psychological thought acknowledges, however, that the human race is not a finished product but a species that is still evolving. Humankind can change, therefore, not only generically but individually. This book is intended to support that view; its aim is to help readers, as present or future partners, to have faith in themselves and in their partners and to believe that people can change, that their relationship can become more loving and harmonious, and they can live together in mutual peace, understanding and love. A certain amount of effort and a great deal of goodwill are needed, but if both partners apply themselves to the task they will find true contentment and at the same time lay the foundations for their children's happiness.

People today have a heightened self-awareness and a new responsibility: complete equality between individuals, regardless of their sex, age, skin colour, religious beliefs, culture or stage of development. In marriage, as in so many other aspects of our social lives, we have not yet learnt to base our everyday dealings upon that new responsibility. The demands it makes on us seem too great for us to hope to meet them without help. Even current scientific knowledge, such as the insights of psychology, is insufficient.

What can we do? We can no longer fall back on familiar habits and traditions. At such times we need God and His word to sustain us. This is the reason for the many scriptural quotations in this book. Science and religion, hand in hand, will lead us to the way of truth, health and maturity of spirit. With them, the couple will be able to blossom and flourish in shared love and trust; in short, in a peaceful partnership.

1

THE WAY THINGS ARE

COUPLES IN CRISIS

The United States and the Soviet Union lead the world in their divorce rates, followed by Germany, Great Britain, France and Switzerland. The number of divorce petitions in England and Wales reached 180,000 a year in the late 1980s. Such statistics do not merely show the steady rise in the number of divorces, but also the accompanying drop in the number of marriages. Thus in Germany, where in the early 1960s one marriage in twelve ended in divorce, the figure had risen by the early 1980s to one in three. In the United States, the number of marriages is barely double the number of divorces, and in Britain four out of ten of today's marriages are likely to fail.

Faced with a situation like this, experts and politicians alike are forced to admit defeat. Governments are baffled, vacillating between the differing explanations put forward by sociology and demography to explain this phenomenon. They end up appointing commissions to examine the possible causes.

HOW DID THINGS GET SO BAD?

I believe there are four main reasons. Examining these in greater detail can help us understand the problems facing the institution of marriage today, and enable us to overcome them in our own marriages.

Resistance to change

Most people today do not believe an individual can change his or her basic attitudes and opinions. 'I am what I am, and that's that' is a common response. They cannot imagine any possibility of modifying their behaviour.

'I can't help it – that's the way I am', they say; or 'I'm the sort of person who . . .' What they do not realize is that statements like this are primarily excuses for continuing bad habits. Such an attitude is therefore very convenient. If that's the way you're made, and if change is impossible, what point is there in trying to reform? Why not save yourself the trouble of trying? And it is true that people who have plenty of courage and energy to devote to changing the world around them, are often noticeably reluctant to try to change themselves.

The majority of the patients who bring their personal problems to a psychotherapist show the same prejudice. This reluctance to change does not make their treatment any easier, of course, because the primary source of all their problems lies within themselves. We are all our own worst enemies.

Lack of faith

Another problem affecting marriage today is lack of faith. By faith I mean firmly held religious belief. What, then, of faith nowadays? All the major faiths, from the Roman Catholic Church, by way of the Orthodox and Protestant Churches, to Islam, Buddhism and Hinduism, are faced with declining congregations and waning influence. They bewail not only their own failure to provide a firm lead, but also the dwindling of religious belief among their followers.

In 1986 an article appeared in a daily newspaper about a survey of the religious attitudes of top management in two large towns. The survey showed that barely twenty per cent of the people involved in the survey unreservedly attributed the role of moral guidance to the Church. Sixty per cent considered that neither Church nor faith was necessary to a morally upright life. When these people were asked, 'To whom do you feel responsible for your actions?', sixty-six per cent named their own family, then their consciences, then themselves. For fourteen per cent God only appeared in fourth place on the list, followed by the community in fifth place. Not one of the 550 people interviewed felt any responsibility towards the Church; in fact sixty-four per cent completely rejected the idea of such a responsibility.

It is not for me to investigate the possible causes of this lack of faith. Let me simply state that this apparent decline in religious belief may be associated with the negative aspects of religion: in-fighting and theological disputes, intolerance and even war in the name of religion. There is also a tendency for large religious organizations to break up and form splinter groups: there were 20,800 Christian sects alone listed in the 1982 edition of the World Christian Encyclopedia. Among the new sects there is a remarkable proliferation of groups directed towards young people, accompanied by a growing preoccupation with 'psi' phenomena: spiritualism, the occult, astrology,

UFOs, exorcism, witchcraft, astral projection, reincarnation and so on. Well may it be said that religious faith is on the decline nowadays.

How does a decline in religious faith affect divorce statistics? Firstly, all religious traditions assert the sanctity of marriage and thus create a firm expectation in the mind of a believer that both she and her partner are committed to a lasting relationship. A long-term commitment is one of the best foundations a marriage can have. Knowing that her partner has faith in the relationship and is not poised to abandon ship at the first sign of rough weather gives confidence and security to a relationship and ensures it is nurtured in a trusting and encouraging environment.

Moreover, religious faith, as we shall see in Chapter 5, assists the individual in her spiritual development and helps her to become less self-centred and more other-centred, which has a unifying effect on the marital relationship. This is also associated with a belief in the human ability to change. When we believe that people can change, we are able to regard our partner and our problems in a more positive and optimistic light and, as a result, will be more prepared to work at our marriages. Thus religious faith can play an important role in strengthening marriages.

Faulty education

While educational facilities and teaching methods vary from country to country, mediocre standards are practically universal. Almost all governments seem to agree on their priorities: education occupies a very low position in their budgets compared with, for example, defence. On an individual level, people tend to spend more on alcohol, cigarettes and drugs, which can damage their health, than they do on education and improving their minds.

Most importantly, education everywhere pays too much attention to filling minds with information whilst at the same time too little importance is placed on those values and skills that would help people to live peacefully together. We must speak out against violence and sow the seeds of peace in the receptive minds of our children and teach them how peace can triumph over violence. We need to surround them with an atmosphere of peace and show them examples of the wonderful things peace can do. Let peace be their dream, their goal, the driving force of their lives.

As well as taking care of her unborn baby's physical well-being, every expectant mother should focus her thoughts on her child's spiritual development. After the birth the most important aspect of the child's upbringing should be the spiritual one. The child must be taught to feel and give pleasure, to share in the joys and sorrows of others, and to treat other people with sensitivity, courtesy and respect. Consequently, at school as in the home, the acquisition of knowledge should take second place to the child's spiritual development and the teaching of spiritual principles.

The way we are educated – at home and at school – clearly has an important effect on our future relationships, because it influences our attitudes and values and the way we relate to our fellow human beings. It seems to me that the question to ask is not so much 'Why do couples split up?' as 'What are we doing to prepare our children to live together in love and harmony?' The way of peace is best taken early in life.

Social equality

The fourth issue is social equality. The notion that every human being has *equal worth* seems to express this point more accurately than the frequently used phrases 'equal rights' or 'equal opportunities'.

The equality I am talking about here is not only equality in relation to the law of the land, but equal rights and responsibilities in human terms. Everyone is entitled to expect the same fair and equitable treatment, respect, consideration, dignity, education and access to information; to work and to share in every aspect of human life. All human beings are entitled to aspire to freedom, love, happiness and peace; to obey their own consciences and to lead their own spiritual lives; to follow their own personal aims and aspirations. Every human being is entitled to every one of these things, because they are a prerequisite of social equality and an expression of the concept that all people are equally valuable and precious, simply because they are human.

Let me repeat: everyone has equal worth as a human being. But of course individual rights may vary according to a person's function within a group. For example, a father who comes home from work at midday is entitled to decide what time the family should have lunch. As an employee he is part of an organization that gives him an hour for lunch and needs him back at a certain time. His little boy, playing with his building bricks, does not have the same right to influence family mealtimes because, unlike his father, he can break off at any time without affecting anyone else. However, the basic right of the child to play is every bit as fundamental as the father's right to work – and when he is older and comes home from school at midday he too will have some say in family mealtimes.

These individual rights that relate to the different functions of family or group members, however, are not as significant as the basic human rights, and it is vital that they are not assigned different values, as in the past, for example, all men's rights were given priority over women's.

Marriage is a partnership in which two individuals of opposite sexes but equal worth as human beings choose to live together as equals. This statement may seem self-evident. It is not, however, the traditional view of marriage. How many adults can look back on their own parents' marriage as an equal partnership? Examples of such true equality in the marriages of previous generations are few and far between.

Because we do not have personal experience of equality in marriage, it falls to the lot of every couple to work things out in their own way. Is it surprising, then, that so many couples fail and give up the struggle? The relative novelty of the concept of equal partnership, and the difficulties that couples experience in trying to achieve it, are prime causes of the rising divorce rate and the general lack of confidence in marriage as a way of life. The proof of this is clearly seen in the fact that two generations ago, in ninety per cent of divorces and separations, it was the man who initiated proceedings. Only in ten per cent of cases did the woman set things in motion. In the next generation the figures were fifty-fifty. Today, in eighty per cent of cases it is the woman who wants to leave her husband.

Until very recently, society was entirely on the side of men and their time-honoured privileges, and women meekly accepted the inferior role assigned to them. Today society has recognized the necessity for and justice of equal rights for women. Conscious of both their equality and their new legal rights, women are refusing to accept a subordinate role and are opting for individual freedom. As often happens, social custom is lagging behind legislation. That is why so many marriages are in trouble today: the law says the partners are equal, but society still expects the wife to take time off work to look after a sick child or wait for the repairman to fix the washing machine, and women frequently shoulder the double burden of housework and a job. The reason the pendulum has possibly swung too far in the opposite direction is that women have been much quicker to see and respond to these new changes than their husbands, and in some cases they have begun to assert their new-found power in much the same negative way as men would have done.

A study of the sacred texts of the major religions can lead to misunderstandings on this subject. Some readers may find passages in them that seem to justify masculine privilege: 'Wives, be subject to your husbands', and so on. In examining these passages, which usually reflect the social practices of the time (similar passages from the Bible enjoin slaves to give entire obedience to their masters!), we ought not to lose sight of the higher, purer principle of equality between men and women.

Of course there are undeniable differences between men and women. Few women can compete with men in physical strength, and no man has ever suckled a child. These differences in certain abilities and functions do not, however, imply a difference in worth as human beings. Thus it is that both partners have equal rights to express their opinions, which neither partner has any right to overrule from some preconceived notion of superiority. Above all, it is important to bear in mind that when consulting or making decisions together as a couple, there will be no simple majority to ensure fairness. Each couple must therefore take pains to ensure both husband and wife have an equal say in the affairs of the family. Again, one partner may deserve special consideration by virtue of particular skills or additional knowledge, but this consideration does not affect anyone's overall worth as an individual, and neither should habitually overrule the other.

We live today in a stage of transition, when the traditional roles of men and women in society are changing, and these changes are having a profound impact on marriage. As women juggle full-time work outside the home with their traditional responsibilities of child-rearing and housework within it, stresses will be felt, and stereotypical divisions of labour will have to be adjusted between husband and wife. Every couple today must negotiate these new challenges, and find its own way of living together as two equals in a harmonious and sustainable relationship.

The promotion of women to their new position of equality is not, therefore, a mere matter of fair play within the law. It goes far beyond that. It entails the establishment of a whole new set of relationships between human beings; relationships based not on tradition or physical strength but on mutual rights, responsibilities and friendship. Only in this way can we function fully as human beings and enjoy a rich and rewarding life within marriage, with husband and wife walking side by side, and neither partner lagging behind.

2

WHAT CAN WE DO?

Every time we undertake a task we must examine what tools we have to hand. That is the only way of distinguishing between what is possible and realistic and what is not. If we fail to do this, we may find ourselves chasing shadows, doomed to failure from the very start.

The problem-solving tools we have at our disposal consist first of all of the functions and faculties of life itself, such as growth, continuity of the species, movement and the receiving of information with our five outer senses (sight, hearing, taste, smell and touch), as well as the emotions. Some of these functions and faculties are confined to humankind. We process incoming information by means of our intellect: intelligence, imagination, thought and memory. Then we progress to action, intuition, active learning, recognition, loving and dreaming.

Finally we come to decision-making, the ability to choose from several possibilities and decide on a course of action. As decision-making plays such a vital role in our lives, and represents a tremendous strength that people generally underestimate, it is this function that we will now examine at length.

DECISION-MAKING

In the past, traditional psychology has delineated only four typical human functions, namely thinking, feeling, willing and acting. However, since what is commonly called the 'will' has led to various misunderstandings, Individual Psychology prefers to talk about decision-making as the third mental function. For example, people talk of being 'strong-willed' or 'weak-willed', or of having or lacking 'will-power'. This led them to talk along the lines of 'I know smoking is bad for my health, but I haven't the will-power to stop'. Supposed lack of will-power offered an easy explanation and a handy excuse for refusing to make the effort to do something. This idea joined forces with the excuse 'I can't help it – that's the way I am', noted in Chapter 1.

The truth is that we are decision-making human beings; by and large we do what we want to do. If we act like animals or children, following our whims and fancies, it is because we have decided to do this, even if we are unwilling or unable to acknowledge the fact. Every action demands a decision. What matters is to be aware of our decision-making, and to learn to make our decisions more *consciously*. Think of a sailing ship: the rudder guides the ship and the wind propels it. Without wind, the ship cannot move forward at all; without the rudder, it cannot be steered. In the same way, while our environment may influence our lives, it is our own decisions that determine what we will make of our experiences, and ultimately of life.

It is important to realize that people today use their decision-making skills almost completely unconsciously. We do not clearly understand our thought processes, which feelings or emotions we use, what actions or patterns of behaviour we resort to. If we have the impression that external forces are controlling our lives, it is because we have chosen to allow them to do so. To be sure, not all of our everyday actions require conscious thought: we do some things automatically, so successfully that to think about them would only interfere with their smooth performance. If we constantly had to stop and make decisions, we would hardly have time to act upon them all. It is therefore only reasonable that much of what we do is automatic. An experienced driver approaching a bend does not make a conscious decision to change down into third gear. He does not need to decide to put his hand on the gear lever, his left foot on the clutch and his right foot on the brake. All these decisions, and countless others, are made automatically. If we had to think hard about all our everyday actions, we would never get around to doing anything. How often do we get up, wash, dress and make breakfast, all on automatic pilot, while we plan the day's activities?

On the other hand, we would benefit from making certain decisions more consciously, which might harm ourselves or others if made without sufficient thought. Take the case of a mother who gives way to an outburst of anger at her child's annoying behaviour. Repeated misbehaviour in children is nearly always a provocation. The mother's impulsive reaction is exactly what the child was looking for; the mother, in reacting in this way, far from taking command of the situation, has put herself in the child's power: it is his game, and they are going to play it according to his rules.

In our relationships with other people we must realize that impulsive reactions like this only aggravate a situation. Moreover, we are not mere responders to external stimuli. This may be hard for us to accept, but in fact no

24

one can annoy us – we create our own feelings of annoyance, however unconsciously. In reality, all our actions and reactions come from within us. People do not readily subscribe to this view, because in doing so they lose an easy excuse for the negative emotions that so often damage their relationships. If we accept that our emotions, which are socially destructive feelings, come from within us, we can no longer hold other people responsible for them. This realization, moreover, enables us to progress from merely reacting to consciously acting. In so doing we regain control of a situation in which we were previously helpless, and we cease to be the victims of circumstances; we have won back our inner freedom. By becoming actors rather than reactors, we assert our independence from others, and learn to direct our own lives.

Most people today are very suspicious of anything they regard as a threat to their independence. That is because, in childhood and adolescence, we were constantly being told what to do. As a result of this, we become sensitive to situations where it looks as if others are trying to control us. True independence, however, is the state people reach when their conscious mind dominates and overcomes their negative impulses, emotions and feelings. By using our inner freedom to decide more consciously, we cease to be slaves of our emotions and become their masters. From there we can move by degrees away from these negative feelings, towards really positive, loving ones. Freed from our destructive impulses, we achieve true spontaneity.

Here is an everyday example. A man comes home late for dinner. He wants to kiss his wife and explain why he was unable to get home on time. But she turns away in annoyance: she has been anxious, she is upset, and she refuses to listen to his explanations. He knows the delay wasn't of his making and his wife's reaction seems

25

thoroughly unfair. So he gets cross too, and their evening is ruined.

If he had been more aware, the husband would not have allowed himself to react angrily to his wife's reproachful behaviour, and he would not have decided to become angry too. He could have sympathized with and accepted his wife's feelings, listened calmly to her reproaches, made a fuss of her and thus softened her anger and encouraged her to behave more reasonably. She in turn, having looked forward to her husband's return, did not have to decide to be angry at his lateness. She could have decided to trust her husband more and, instead of fuming at his delay, spent the time doing something useful and enjoyable, such as reading a good book.

This may seem rather unrealistic to some readers, but the strength that lies behind such changes in behaviour patterns is probably the greatest strength we humans can draw on. It is the strength of belief.

THE POWER OF BELIEF

By belief I do not mean only religious faith, although faith is certainly the noblest expression of all human beliefs. What I am talking about here is something more general, a typical human function on a par with thinking or feeling.

It is a function we use continuously throughout the day, though not necessarily on a conscious level, for we need to *believe* in something before we act on it. Belief thus conditions most of our actions, even if we ourselves are unaware of this. To use a simple example, readers of this book would not read it if they did not believe they could learn something, or benefit in some way from it. Whatever we do, we do because we believe it is right or useful or necessary.

One of the most important forms of belief is belief in self, what we might call courage or self-confidence. It is a kind of appetite for enterprise, a readiness to confront difficulties and take action. If courage is belief in oneself the opposite of courage could be described as lack of belief in oneself, as uncertainty, a sense of inferiority, and being prey to fears and inhibitions. This lack of courage and self-confidence is often associated with perfectionism. Perfectionists set themselves impossible standards. They identify themselves with everything they do, and if what they do is not good enough, they feel that they themselves cannot be much good either.

Perfectionists think they are not allowed to make any mistakes, or that an error would mean the end of the world. They cannot admit their mistakes and try to conceal them from everyone, even from themselves. Consequently, they find an excuse for every mistake they make. All people who lack courage and self-esteem want so desperately to be right, and wonder why they often find themselves in conflict with others. Every argument, be it large or small, happens when one person who wants to be right meets another person with the same aim. Lack of belief in oneself and in life in general also leads to pessimism and other negative traits, one of the commonest being fear of responsibility.

Nothing is more widespread today than the mistrust of, or lack of belief in, other people, which stems from lack of confidence, of belief in oneself. When we do not believe in other people, we cease to regard them as friends and equals, and they become competitors. We project our own negative thoughts and feelings onto them. All kinds of problems can result from this, such as difficulty in making contact with other people, which can lead to veiled or open aggression. Or perhaps we do make contact, but we do so in a superficial way that gives no opportunity for a real exchange of feelings and ideas, and we are impoverished by our failure to relate well to other people.

It is important for parents to believe in their children; if they do not, they will discourage them and destroy their self-confidence. Spoiling and pampering children is a reflection of parents' lack of belief in their children, which both stunts their courage and independence, and teaches them to be self-centred. These problems are at the root of most child-rearing difficulties.

Lack of belief in one's partner leads to all sorts of tensions in the marital relationship, including jealousy, which is the bitter fruit of lack of belief in oneself.

Lack of belief in our communal responsibility to society leads to social problems such as strikes, corruption, crime and terrorism, rebellion and revolution. Lack of trust between races or nations leads to problems such as the cold war and armed stalemate in the shadow of the bomb. When people no longer believe in nature, in the earth, in the whole of God's creation, they cease to respect it. The results of such an attitude can be seen worldwide. We need only mention the word pollution. How long do we have left before our destructiveness and neglect have made our world uninhabitable?

Those who do not believe sufficiently in life, often believe in enjoyment too much. If you have no aim in life, what use is there in living? Fill up this pointless, aimless life of yours with pleasure – alcohol and drugs will help you! To such people, study and work seem a tedious obligation instead of a blessing. They have lost their goal, and in doing so have lost their sense of identity: for we are what we aspire to. To them life becomes meaningless, and they lose their belief in the future. Hope withers and dies, to be replaced by anxiety. Jesus said:

28

'I bid you, put away anxious thoughts about food and drink to keep you alive, and clothes to cover your body. Surely life is more than food, the body more than clothes . . . Is there a man of you who by anxious thought can add a foot to his height? . . . Set your mind on God's kingdom and His justice before everything else, and all the rest will come to you as well. So do not be anxious about tomorrow; tomorrow will look after itself.'[2]

When shall we read the signs of our times? When shall we understand that we are being called to live not only with a heightened awareness, but also in a more 'spiritual' way? What does leading a spiritual life mean? We shall look at this in more detail in a later chapter. However, practically everyone accepts that the materialism and selfishness that hold sway today represent the opposite of spirituality. Many of us believe that life is pregnant with a new promise and a new hope; that human horizons will not be forever limited to the quest for money and material goods.

Sometimes, materialism stems from past or present poverty, as in eastern Europe and the developing countries of the Third World. Sometimes it is the result of a surfeit of good things, as in the rich countries of the West. Humankind continues to display the mentality of famine, even when we are able to provide for everyone. When all our needs have been met, as in Europe today, we still go on inventing new requirements from force of habit – until we realize that we are walking down a blind alley. Then we see that the only viable route to a worthwhile life lies in a balance between materialism and spirituality. We can see a similar development in the sexual aspect of our lives. Sexual love without spirituality is empty and meaningless, and has led to the modern trend of blatant sexuality in our society.

Human beings can misuse anything if they choose, even their own beliefs. It is possible to believe in something too strongly and unquestioningly. One example would be placing all one's faith in science. Science is a fine and noble thing, but it is often surrounded by superstitious nonsense, and the unreasonable expectation that it can solve all humanity's problems. The great philosopher and religious teacher 'Abdu'l-Bahá said:

'Religion and science are the two wings upon which man's intelligence can soar into the heights, with which the human soul can progress. It is not possible to fly with one wing alone! Should a man try to fly with the wing of religion alone he would quickly fall into the quagmire of superstition, whilst on the other hand, with the wing of science alone he would also make no progress, but fall into the despairing slough of materialism.'[3]

Let us shun fanaticism in both religion and science: each balances, tempers and complements the other. Each has its place in the scheme of things. Science provides the means, but only religion provides the direction, the aim.

Let us end with two more examples of the misuse of belief. Many people put too much faith in the law and not enough in human beings. To them, laws are more important than people. They forget that the law was created to serve people, not the other way round. There are also those who believe that aggression and war are the best way of obtaining advantages or settling disagreements. They still have not realized that conflict and war lead only to yet more conflict and war.

The importance of belief as a human function is seen in the pervasiveness of negative belief – or belief in the negative – today, from which few of us are completely free. This is fear, the belief in something hostile or threatening, or in our own failings and future failures. Such fear, too, is a way of denying the positive in life and the powers of love and truth; ultimately it represents a lack of belief in God. Sadly, just as violence only breeds violence, fear traps us in a vicious circle. It serves to focus our attention on our weaknesses, on the very thing we want to avoid, which in turn only discourages us further and leads to even greater fears of failure.

THE WORD OF GOD

The greatest power in creation is the Word of God. He created us and all the universe around us, and all His awesome power is revealed to us, and is accessible to us, through His Word. We can read God's Word in the teachings of His messengers and the founders of His religions. Bahá'u'lláh asserts:

> 'O friend of mine! The Word of God is the king of words and its pervasive influence is incalculable. It hath ever dominated and will continue to dominate the realm of being. The Great Being saith: The Word is the master key for the whole world, inasmuch as through its potency the doors of the hearts of men, which in reality are the doors of heaven, are unlocked.'[4]

However, people who do not believe in God are unable to make use of this power. They content themselves with all the available powers of science and technology, powers that are all dependent on human beings.

The Word of God is found in the Holy Scriptures of all people. Around the world, most people follow a religion, the writings of a founder of a religion or writings that have been handed down and are recognized as holy. The contents of these holy writings are, in part at least, known to the believers, and a large proportion of them concern how the believers should lead their lives, how they can live in accordance with God's will. If everyone lived according to the principles, rules and recommendations of their religion, then we would probably have peace on earth today. For the prerequisite of peace is unity and all the major religions agree that the real rules for living rest on the love of God and the love of one's neighbour.

But since we only partly base our lives on these regulations, the contents of the Holy Scriptures seem to be more theory than practice for most people. What stops us from moving from theory to practice? We could describe it as a lack of courage or, to put it simply, as fear. Both mean that we do not believe strongly enough. Consequently it is important for us to strengthen our religious belief by becoming more aware of the function of belief in general, and by using it more positively and more spiritually.

3

TOWARDS A MORE CONSCIOUS LIFE

CHOOSING TO BE CONSCIOUS

Psychologists today are virtually unanimous in their estimate that human beings use only ten to fifteen per cent of their mental capacity. Of course this statement has its reassuring side, because it shows how much scope for improvement there is, both for ourselves and for our descendants. At the same time, however, it puts us under an obligation to set to work, training our minds towards a higher level of consciousness.

The word 'conscious' is an adjective used to describe something, and that is how we are using it here. Several schools of thought have used 'conscious' and its opposite, 'unconscious', as nouns with 'the unconscious' playing an important role. This could lead some people to regard it as an entity, a power outside our conscious control and not subject to our influence. The consequence of such a viewpoint is the potential misuse of this concept, invoking it to excuse our inaction or sense of powerlessness in the face of our shortcomings. True, there are some aspects of our mental life of which we are wholly or partly unconscious. But this is the result of insufficient education, experience, information or awareness on our part. Or perhaps we are unwilling to admit to our mistakes or bad behaviour and prefer to forget them.

Of course, not being conscious of certain things can have its positive side, as we saw with the motorist in Chapter 2. We know that some actions are performed more smoothly on automatic pilot, without conscious thought, than if we considered them carefully step by step. However, important as it is to try to become more conscious, we should not be perfectionists. We will never achieve 100% consciousness, and in this, as in so many other aspects of life, perfectionism is a pitfall to avoid. As is so often the case with objectives, it is not so important to reach the goal as to try to use it as a signpost to follow, in this case a signpost to greater consciousness.

The story that follows is told of the Prophet Muhammad. It shows us that we should try to recognize as many aspects of reality as possible. One day, as He approached a town, Muhammad saw a man riding to meet Him. It was one of the few disciples He had in that town. The man greeted his leader.

'I have come to warn you that there is no point in your visiting this town. Its inhabitants are not only ignorant and stupid, but wicked and cruel too. They don't want anything to do with you or your teachings. They will only give you trouble. You'd best make a detour and avoid this town altogether.'

'Yes', replied Muhammad, 'you are right, my son. Thank you for warning me.' Nevertheless He rode on towards the town.

A little while later, He saw a second rider coming to meet Him. The second man greeted Him, full of joy and feverish with eagerness.

'The whole town is looking forward to your arrival.

They can hardly believe their good fortune. You'll love them – they're marvellous people! They need you and you'll be able to help them so much.'

Once again, Muhammad thanked him, saying: 'Yes, you are right, my son.'

After this messenger left, one of Muhammad's travelling companions spoke to Him.

'Master', he said, 'I don't understand. These two men have brought you conflicting reports, and yet you told both of them that they were right. This cannot be: a thing cannot be both black and white at the same time.'

The Prophet replied: 'Oh, but it can. From his own point of view, each messenger was right. But each of them could see only a part of the truth, not the whole truth.'

The following points will help us to become more conscious and to apply all our faculties and strengths more effectively in the pursuit of a loving understanding between partners.

IDENTIFYING OUR GOALS

Everything we decide to feel, think, perceive, believe and do has a motive, a goal of some kind, even if we ourselves have no clear understanding of what we are aiming for. Where our mental and emotional life is concerned, we need to ask 'What is this leading to?' rather than 'Why are we doing this?' We always manage to come up with reasons and explanations aplenty, especially when it comes to making excuses. But few of us are used to examining our own aims and motives closely, to looking for the intention, the goal, of our behaviour.

Each of us pursues both positive and negative goals. For example, we would all like to achieve our full potential and we all try, consciously or otherwise, to reach that goal, the goal of perfection. Religious people strive to come closer to God. Companionship is another goal; nobody is really happy alone, even if they seem resigned to loneliness. Everyone strives for security, certainty and a sense of belonging to someone or something. In this context, even the so-called 'drives', such as self-preservation or preservation of the species, must be considered as goals.

All these goals are natural and perfectly acceptable, pursued in a positive way. The question to ask ourselves is: 'What am I doing to reach my goal?' Then: 'Is my goal positive or negative?' Negative goals are the ones that may hurt other people or, worst of all, can only be attained at the expense of others. We pay dearly for such goals; whether we attain them or not, they still lead to failure. It doesn't matter whether we acknowledge our failure or claim it as a victory: we may have an A in Business, but we still have an E in Life. Among these negative goals we need to differentiate between short-term and long-term goals. Long-term goals are deeply rooted in our earliest childhood and we may be almost completely unconscious of them, or at least not sufficiently conscious of them to understand what they really mean to our lives.

Long-term goals

Let us pass over the short-term goals for the moment, and list some of today's commonest long-term goals. Naturally, this list is far from being definitive – human invention is inexhaustible in this, as in other matters – but here are some examples:

I want to be big . . .

I want everybody to say how good I am . . .

I want people to like me . . .

I want to be the centre of attention . . .

I want everybody to admit that I'm right . . .

I want to be in control; I don't want to be pushed around . . .

I have to keep up my defences, because other people are not to be trusted . . .

I have to fight others to get what I desire . . .

I want to be better than everybody else . . .

I want to be morally superior . . .

I need a strong man to protect me . . .

I want to manipulate and use other people and make them help me . . .

I want life to be exciting . . .

I want to be rich . . .

I want to live in comfort . . .

I want to suffer, so that I can look down on my oppressors . . .

I want to get the most out of life . . .

To make long-term goals less negative and more positive usually requires the help of a psychotherapist. In general these goals are so deeply entrenched in our minds, and we have had so much practice in striving for them, that changing them calls for more faith and courage than most people possess. The mere desire to turn over a new leaf presupposes a self-awareness and self-dissatisfaction that constitute the beginning of a change from within; but only belief, powerful and consciously trained, can transform negative goals into more positive ones.

Short-term goals

On the other hand, we can all learn to modify our short-term goals, especially as there are only five basic short-term goals that lead to anti-social or potentially harmful behaviour. Here, then, are the five negative short-term goals:

1. We want to excuse the shortcomings we have – or think we have.
2. We want attention or to be comforted.
3. We want to feel superior or, at least, not to be inferior.
4. We want to take revenge for something.
5. We want to withdraw.

If we want to modify these goals, the first step is to discover which one is being pursued in a particular situation. Once we have identified the right goal, we can then ask ourselves whether, in a similar situation, we would still feel the need to pursue it. Usually we find that recognizing our goal allows us to see through our actions, and the moment we do this we will be much less likely to want to achieve the same goal with the same negative behaviour in the future.

Tackling our short-term goals can make a very important contribution to our efforts to improve our relationships with others, and is a wonderful way of achieving greater peace with our partners. Let us take a closer look at these goals in the context of some everyday situations:

Mr A finds his wife has bought a fancy window-cleaning gadget from a door-to-door salesman 'because she couldn't say no'. She has done this sort of thing several times before. Mr A flies into a fury. Such a reaction suggests that he is using his anger, unconsciously, as a way of reaching a goal. Which goal?

Goal 1. Mr A could be looking for *an excuse* because he feels guilty about not earning enough. He is trying to saddle his wife with all the responsibility for his financial problems.

Goal 2. Perhaps he wants *attention* because he feels his wife does not take enough notice of him.

Goal 3. A desire to demonstrate his *superiority* may be his goal, because he takes pride in his thriftiness. 'I scrimp and save and look what you do with my money!'

Goal 4. He may want *revenge*; he feels his wife does not listen to him enough and resolves to spoil her day with his recriminations.

Goal 5. He wants to *withdraw* and sulk. 'She's incorrigible – I give up!'

In order to come to a more decisive identification of the goal responsible in this particular situation, we must also look at Mrs A's reaction, then at her husband's response. If she responds to his angry reproaches by reacting guilt-ily, for example, we can infer that Mr A has goal 1 in mind. He is using her action as an excuse for not earning enough money, and makes her an equally guilty party in their lack of funds.

If, on the other hand, she soothes his anger with kisses, Mr A was probably in pursuit of goal 2. He wants atten-tion; she provides it. Goal 3 is indicated if Mrs A reacts angrily to her husband's scolding: she resents being placed in an inferior position. If his wife has to put up with endless reproaches, Mr A had goal 4 – revenge – in mind. What if, having a better way with words, she looks like winning the argument, and he retreats to his room and sulks? Then we can be sure Mr A had goal 5 in mind. All this may seem very complicated. In reality it is quite simple, because over the years we tend to use the same behaviour to achieve a particular goal. The scenario may vary; the basic aims do not.

And what about Mrs A? Her inability to say 'no' to the salesman indicates personal insecurity. She wants to be liked – that is one of her long-term goals. But she is also likely to be pursuing one of the five short-term goals, perhaps goal 3 or goal 4.

Here is another example: Mrs B gets furious with her husband practically every day because, despite frequent requests to use the laundry basket, he keeps leaving his dirty clothes lying around. She could be using her anger to pursue any of the five short-term goals.

If she is aiming for goal 1, she is probably looking for an excuse for her own lack of tidiness. It could be attention-seeking behaviour, goal 2, if Mr B helps her to feel better about his untidiness, or if he promises to be tidier in future. We could recognize a need to feel superior, goal 3, if an argument ensues. If goal 4 is her aim, she will get her revenge by making Mr B's life a misery all day long. Goal 5 will lead Mrs B to retire into a corner and refuse to have anything further to do with him.

Let us take a jealous partner as our third example. Jealousy usually indicates a lack of self-confidence. For one reason or another, one partner is unsure of his or her personal worth – 'Am I good enough for him/her?'. Here is an example of such feelings. At a dance, Mr C demonstrates a certain disregard for his wife in dancing closely – and frequently – with women younger than her, and she becomes jealous.

What form will Mrs C's jealousy take? Will she be bad-tempered, reproach her husband, or make a scene, either in public or in private? Or will she become depressed and withdrawn? It all depends on her goal.

Here is one last example to demonstrate how we use our feelings to help us achieve our goal. Today most people still act according to the so-called 'pleasure principle'. This means that we prefer to do only what we want to do and leave important jobs undone simply because we do not feel like tackling them. We also use postponement to get out of doing things, putting off unavoidable tasks again and again, until it is almost too late to do them at all. What excuse do we use for this negligence? 'I didn't want to . . . I just didn't feel like doing it.' As if wanting or not wanting to do something were some immutable law of nature!

However, people decide everything that they do or do not do, whether consciously or not, and this realisation can be applied to a particular situation like a formula. This is how it works: First I tell myself that if I do not feel like doing something, it is because I have made up my mind not to, since a person does what he wants to do. I have to accept this decision of mine because nothing in the world can make me want to do it, except a conscious decision of my own to find pleasure in doing it. Next I must observe myself to find out what I really want to do. Which is stronger, my unconscious decision not to feel like doing this task, or my conscious decision to do what I have to do, and get it over with? This process of analysis can help me to tackle the essential things.

However if, in spite of everything, I still do not feel like doing the job, I can go on to the next method to try to find out exactly why I am so reluctant to act. Obviously my unconscious decision not to feel pleasure in doing something is stronger than the conscious decision to do it. This means it seems more advantageous to me. The advantage – so far unconscious to me – lies in the fact that my lack of pleasure enables me to pursue one or more of the five short-term goals that we have just examined. Perhaps, with the help of my unconscious decision not to feel like doing something, I am looking for an excuse for something I feel guilty about (goal 1). Am I seeking someone's attention – my partner's, for example, in obliging him/her to remind me of my duty (goal 2)? Or am I seeking to achieve a sense of superiority, or avoid a feeling of inferiority, in showing my partner that I don't take orders from anybody (goal 3)? Or again, some resentment may be prompting me to seek revenge against my partner by ruining his or her day (goal 4). Or perhaps I decide to withdraw into myself and sulk, and make myself unavailable to my family (goal 5).

When I have used this process of elimination to recognize the true goal behind my reluctance to act, the goal loses its power over me. I will no longer be able to use the negative behaviour to pursue it as strongly as before. Moreover, as soon as I understand my motives, I may also make up my mind to change my behaviour. It will then be possible for me to decide to tackle the unavoidable task, and even to enjoy doing it in the process. The technique, therefore, is to drag the goals that motivate us into the full light of reason. Only such conscious recognition can bring about a change in our behaviour because it then becomes impossible to deceive ourselves any longer.

If this approach does not succeed, either we have wrongly diagnosed the short-term goal, or the culprit is one or more of our long-term goals, such as those set out on page 37. Most of these long-term goals are too deeply buried, too far out of reach of conscious thought, for us to change them without recourse to psychotherapy or at least some specialist knowledge, although we should be able to recognize some of them. By self-examination and other methods of personal education, we can therefore make some progress towards self-knowledge.

The first step is to realize that behind our not wanting to do something may lie perfectionist goals such as 'I must do everything to a very high standard' or 'I cannot allow myself to make mistakes'. This recognition does not usually bring immediate results, but is part of the process of self-discovery. And when we are able to bring emotions into this process, we can begin to make real progress. Self-development starts when, feeling some surge of negative emotion – anger for example – we are able to view it with a certain wry irony. 'Oh dear', we say to ourselves. 'Here we go again!' From the moment we can laugh at ourselves, we cease to take ourselves, or our feelings, so seriously. This is a reliable indication that we are getting to know ourselves. Good humour and the ability to laugh at ourselves are the surest signs of well-being and inner freedom.

DEVELOPING A POSITIVE ATTITUDE

Nothing in this world is wholly negative. Above all, no human being is altogether bad. Therefore we can resolve to look only at the positive aspects in everything and to notice only the good and worthwhile qualities in everyone. The negative has no existence in its own right. It is merely the absence of something positive. I can bring light into a dark room, but I cannot make a bright room dark. The most I can do is turn off or cover the light. In the same way, evil has no existence other than as the absence of good.

We must add a new, more tolerant concept to the either-

or dualism of the past. Instead of 'It's got to be either black or white,' we must learn to say, like Muhammad in the story related earlier in this chapter, 'Why not both?' In other words, we must get used to seeing people and things in all their rich diversity and adapting to differences that may begin by offending or shocking us but end by enriching us. To do this we will have to develop a more positive attitude.

From childhood on, we are surrounded, at home, at school and at work, by dissatisfied people who view everyone and everything with neither goodwill nor tolerance. As the poet Maria von Ebner-Eschenbach said, 'People today are born fault-finders. All they see of handsome Achilles is his heel.' A Chinese proverb says, 'Do something good and your next-door neighbour will never hear about it. Do something bad and you'll be the talk of the town.'

On the other hand, the poet Ludwig Uhland asked, 'How, my heart, can you lose hope, when even the thorns bear roses?'; the poet Novalis said, 'The higher we rise, the lovelier the earth seems to us'; and another saying is: 'Whoever sees goodness in other people, gazes on them with the eyes of God.'

One of the best-known sayings of the Bahá'í teacher 'Abdu'l-Bahá is:

'To be silent concerning the faults of others, to pray for them, and to help them, through kindness, to correct their faults. To look always at the good and not at the bad. If a man has ten good qualities and one bad one, to look at the ten and forget the one; and if a man has ten bad qualities and one good one, to look at the one and forget the ten.'[5]

Needless to say, overlooking the faults of others does not mean we must fall victim to them. Nor does developing a more positive attitude to others mean becoming blind, but rather entails a refusal to dwell on or tell tales about other people's mistakes. Indeed, when we decide to become more positive, we actually see more; we become more conscious, and can be much more effective in helping people, especially our partners and ourselves, to become more peaceful.

From the many quotations on this important theme, I would like to select a few that clarify the advantages of the positive approach to life: 'Your eye can make the world light or dark; the way you look at it, it will laugh or cry' (the German poet, Friedrich Rueckert), and as Milton noted in *Paradise Lost*, 'The mind is its own place, and in itself can make a Heav'n of Hell, a Hell of Heav'n'.

There are so many good and beautiful things to see and do – why waste our lives mulling over things that are not worth a second glance? It is easier to shoulder your burden than to drag it; it is better to promote good health than to fight against sickness. It is wiser to seek out joy than merely to avoid pain. Let us live hoping for the best, rather than perpetually fearing the worst. But in order to maintain this positive approach to ourselves and to life, we must learn not to take ourselves too seriously, and to face both success and failure with the same good grace and equanimity.

Some may regard this advice as rather old-fashioned, but a story from my work as a psychologist will show where positive and negative attitudes can lead.

A woman with two small children complained of excessive nervousness and sensitivity. She had difficulty in getting on with both her five-year-old daughter and her own mother. When I asked her what she thought her husband liked best about her, she was unable to think of anything. She knew with certainty, however, exactly what he disliked about her.

I asked her to bring her husband along to the next session, and saw him on his own. 'What do you like best about your wife?' I asked. The husband at once reeled off a whole list of excellent qualities. The doctor then asked the wife to come into the room, and told her what her husband had just said about her. Her response was tears of joy: he had found far less fault with her than she had with herself. The couple left the consulting room hand in hand, determined to encourage each other more and to maintain a positive attitude to life. Because the wife felt better about herself, her relationships with her mother and daughter improved immediately.

It is up to us to decide to be positive or negative about life, ourselves or other people. If we develop a positive attitude to ourselves, it helps us to be more creative and to be more positive in our relations with others. And if we approach our fellow human beings with respect, regard, trust and goodwill, it can help them to live up to the positive image we hold of them.

WHAT ARE OUR RESPONSIBILITIES AS A COUPLE?

If we want to become more conscious, we must turn our attention to what Alfred Adler called our 'life tasks',[6] those duties and responsibilities in life that help us better understand the meaning and purpose of our existence. A life without responsibility is a pointless, purposeless sort of life. No couple will stay together very long unless they share the same view of their responsibilities, for shared responsibilities are the cornerstone of married life. Couples must tune their violins together if they want to play in harmony, and the following list of responsibilities or life tasks can be helpful whether couples work on their own or with a counsellor. It is particularly important for couples to discuss these matters in later married life. It is never too early to begin, but clearly the first years of marriage tend to be taken up with such immediate demands as child-rearing and home-making, which pre-occupy younger couples and are the focus of their discussions.

Love, marriage and child-rearing

Work and careers

Friendships and social contacts

Nature and culture: our bodies
the natural world
material things and science
art

Our relationship with ourselves

Religion, morality and our personal philosophy

Love and marriage

God created humankind in two groups, male and female, for the procreation of children and the continuation and development of the human race. Monogamy is the best way of achieving this, which is why all the major religions teach it.

All through the ages, wise people have preached peace and harmony between couples as a prerequisite for a strong and lasting marriage. In the Talmud we read: 'Peace is the basis for happiness in marriage.' And Martin Luther, founder of the sixteenth-century Protestant Reformation, said: 'There is no more loving or friendly or uplifting relationship, community and society than a good marriage, if the couple lives together in peace and unity.'

Meeting the challenge of marriage and building a lasting relationship ought to go hand in hand with fulfilling the second task, namely the responsibility of work, and in former times the two tended to go together. The man, regarded as the future breadwinner of the family, was expected to have completed his training and to have a steady job with a suitable income before even proposing marriage. Nowadays, however, professional training is often a lengthy affair, leaving young people financially dependent on their parents or the state, and in no position to support a family. This comparatively recent development means that few young people are in a financial position to consider marriage until long after puberty.

The only solution that I can see to this dilemma – with its potentially grave moral and social consequences – is to encourage relatively early marriage, and to abandon the concept of the husband as sole breadwinner which, with the new emphasis on the education and training of women, is no longer necessary or realistic. Parents ought to encourage early marriage (obviously, I am not talking about the marriage of under-eighteens here) and to consider it their duty to help a young couple to set up home, and to assist them financially for as long as necessary. This solution would have the advantage of channelling their youthful ardour into a stable, long-lasting relationship, which would solve a lot of the sexual problems that are so rife today.

Work and career

Everybody has a right and a duty to work. Shoghi Effendi puts it very clearly:

'It is the duty of those who are in charge of the organization of society to give every individual the opportunity of acquiring the necessary talent in some kind of profession, and also the means of utilizing such a talent, both for its own sake and for the sake of earning the means of his livelihood. Every individual, no matter how handicapped and limited he may be, is under the obligation of engaging in some work or profession, for work, especially when performed in the spirit of service, is . . . a form of worship. It has not only a utilitarian purpose, but has a value in itself, because it draws us nearer to God, and enables us to better grasp His purpose for us in this world. It is obvious, therefore, that the inheritance of wealth cannot make anyone immune from daily work.'[7]

Friends and social contacts

In every marriage each partner should have friends of his or her own, and they should also have friends in common who are dependable and can be relied on in times of need, and who give richness and warmth to the couple's relationship. Friends are better than acquaintances, who in turn are better than the self-absorption of an isolated, inward-looking couple. Our social interest, which can also be described as our concern for and belief in our fellow human beings, is measured by how we relate to other people, how much we regard them as fellow human beings rather than as competitors. A couple who are interested only in their own concerns will become lonely and socially and emotionally impoverished as time passes.

Friendships do not depend on the time available for social contacts, but on their quality of togetherness and unity, as seen in the affection we give, in our willingness to help each other, in our harmony of thought, in working together, in sharing our hopes and fears, in the joy of togetherness. Friendship requires plenty of patience, understanding and insight in addition to mutual care and encouragement.

Our bodies

If we strive for a more conscious life we must not exclude our bodies, the natural world or the material things that surround us. We should look after our bodies, and here too an agreement between the two partners is helpful. It is all too easy to abuse the body through overwork or idleness, and to disregard its basic needs, such as exercise, fresh air, healthy food in moderation, adequate sleep and rest, and relaxation in peace and quiet.

The body is like a horse or donkey – indeed, St Francis referred to it as Brother Ass – which carries our spirit and personality and must be well looked after to enable it to perform its functions effectively. Or, as Shakespeare put it in *Othello* (Act I, scene iii), 'Our bodies are our gardens, to the which our wills are gardeners.' We should make time for food, exercise and sleep, and pay special attention to our nerves, taking time out for prayer and meditation as well as for real peace and relaxation.

It is very important that the two partners should consult together when there is excessive anxiety about physical

50

problems or when harmful substances such as tobacco, alcohol or drugs are in question. Today everyone knows how dearly our bodies and souls pay for such so-called pleasures, and this is an area where each partner should be concerned for the health of the other and discuss their concerns with them.

The natural world

In recent years there has been a growing realization that our misuse of the natural world is likely to rebound on us with disastrous long-term consequences for humankind as a species and, in the short term, on our health and balance as individuals. We cannot live in isolation: we are part of the living world and we depend on it for our existence. Anything that threatens the natural world is a threat – direct or indirect – to us too. We are part of nature and nature is a part of us.

Let us therefore enjoy nature in all its rich diversity – not only the radiant dawns and glorious sunsets, but the timeless miracle of a blade of grass, a snowflake or an autumn leaf. Understanding nature helps us to understand ourselves. We are the pinnacle of all creation, but that does not give us the right to destroy it. We owe the natural world our interest, our respect, our attention, our love and our care. Only then can we hope to live in harmony with the world around us.

The same applies to the way we treat animals. Of all our contacts with nature, our relationships with animals are the warmest and most spontaneous. Animals *are* nature, in all its primal innocence. Through human contact, domestic animals become humanized; they meet our needs for uncritical devotion and companionable silence. Their calm acceptance of suffering and death is an example to us all. Animals are beautiful and gentle; they gladden the heart and delight the eye. Their speed and agility, their cunning and intuition, their keen senses, are a constant reminder of the wonder and wisdom of nature.

Every home needs an animal. Children especially need a companion, always patient, always available, never too busy to share their games and fantasies, their joys and sorrows; warm, faithful, welcoming, consoling; never criticizing or telling tales: the perfect confidant and friend. And – most vital of all – pets enable children, who always feel to some extent dominated and protected by adults, to assume, by virtue of their superior intelligence, a dominant and protective role themselves, and to accept the consequent responsibility.

However, an animal should not be kept as a mere toy or a replacement for human love. If we do not look after a cat properly, she will not only eat mice, but also birds, useful animals like lizards and frogs, and even our neighbour's goldfish. How often do pet owners think only of their precious darlings, and ignore their responsibility to others? We must be kind and compassionate to animals, but within reason. Naturally, some animals are harmful or dangerous and may need to be kept under control: excessive kindness to a wolf might result in cruelty to a whole flock of sheep; failure to kill a rabid dog might even result in the death of several people. But our whole attitude to the animal world should be governed by respect, compassion and loving kindness. Animals are living allegories for human strengths and weaknesses: they can show us how we, as human beings, should *not* behave as well as demonstrating love and other good qualities. Thus in observing and understanding them, we can learn a great deal about ourselves.

Material things

Matter, which is in itself inanimate, is nevertheless the basis for all living things. That is why it is both very close to us and very remote. Close, because we ourselves are composed of matter and are to a large extent subject to the same natural laws as inanimate objects; remote, because we are alive and sentient and endowed with free will and responsibility. But inanimate things are important for another reason: through our intelligence, we human beings can understand the properties of matter and develop science and technology to harness it either for our own benefit or for our own destruction. Today, more than ever before, we need to learn respect and love if our species is to survive. Let us therefore study material things because they have so much to teach us: geology, geography, astronomy can all show us that there may be an infinite wisdom in the world. Husband and wife can share hobbies like walking, or collecting fossils or stones, and help their children to appreciate the beauty and wonder of the natural world.

Many books are now available to help interested non-specialists understand the principal scientific and technological achievements of today. To live in the age of radio and television, space travel and computers, requires some understanding of how and why things work: it is not enough merely to know which switch to press. We need not be carried along by our peers to the point of excess and 'materialism', but computers and TV have as much a place in our time as books.

Science opens up wide perspectives to the human mind, like the view from a mountain top. Far from trivializing the universe, these perspectives increase our sense of wonderment at the prodigious diversity and complexity of creation. The more we know and understand, the more we recognize the limitedness of our knowledge and the imponderability of the mystery of creation. We become conscious of our own insignificance and of the transience and fragility of our achievements.

Art

Painting, architecture, the cinema, literature or music – all art forms are important. In no other aspect of our lives are the problems of our age so clearly seen. This is because art is a typically human means of expression and the quintessence of human achievements. Art is the manifestation of the overwhelming human need to express something that transcends the material world. We should not exclude even modern art – whatever that might be – from our lives. We do not have to join in the confusion and exaggeration and obscurity, but should try to understand, even if experts find this hard, if only so that we can learn to differentiate real art from other art forms.

Music is almost a divine art, in that it has tremendous power to inspire and uplift us. Children are especially moved by music, and they should be exposed to it in such a way that they learn to love and understand it, and their lives are cheered by it. Through art, people seek out for themselves a new vision, a new way of listening, a new perception of the world and their place in it. More than any other human activity, art can lead us to spiritual things, and it ought to play a major part in our education.

Inner harmony

Now we will turn to the relationship of the individual with him or herself. Although this task has never been

54

more important, it is not the easiest to fulfil. People today are full of inner conflicts; consciously or unconsciously they are at war with themselves. How can we be at peace with our partner – or anyone else – unless we are at peace with ourselves? The only way to peace – with ourselves or with our partner – is through unity. For the individual, this requires an understanding of our purpose in life, and a conscious effort to develop our potential as human beings and play our part in contributing to society. As we will see, the way to unity with our partner lies through frank discussion and consultation, tolerance, mutual respect and a willingness to listen as well as talk. In such conditions differences of opinion add richness, not conflict, to a relationship.

Religion, morality and personal philosophy

Finally, a few words about our most important life task: the responsibility we all have to develop our own philosophy of life and religion. All of us feel the need to give a shape and meaning to the world as we see it and to decide where we stand from the religious point of view. Each must, to some degree, find answers to the three big questions: Where do we come from? Where are we going? Who, if anyone, is out there watching over us?

It is not enough to be born into a particular religion and to join in, through force of habit, the practices we have learnt from our parents, for if we do continue in the creed we were born in, we do so as the result of a decision, even if we are unaware of having made it. It is better to make such decisions and choices consciously, after careful consideration; it is the responsibility of every human being to work out his or her own beliefs and personal philosophy. Each of us must search for truth independently, and this is one of the greatest principles of our times and should be everyone's aim. This search need not be exclusive of others. Indeed, where it includes our partners it will broaden and deepen our relationship and ensure it does not become mired in everyday issues.

4

CHOOSING A PARTNER

The choice of a partner is something many people find
difficult today. The main problem is lack of experience of
successful relationships with members of the other sex
that incorporate our modern expectations of equality,
relationships that embody a real sense of togetherness
where neither dominates the other. There are few reassuring precedents for such relationships, and role models
from earlier generations have become inappropriate. Since
the choice of partner is so critical to a peaceful and harmonious marriage, we must make our choice consciously
and after mature reflection: no spur-of-the-moment
decisions here, or we shall pay very dearly for our mistakes.

LIVING TOGETHER

Lack of faith in our ability to make the right choice and
the fear of discovering that our marriage partners are not,
in the end, suited to be our partners for life, has led to a
lack of faith in the institution of marriage. Nowadays,
more and more couples are living together outside marriage. In 1970 there were 523,000 such couples in the

United States of America. By 1984 the number had grown to two million. The reason people most commonly give is the fear that the other person may not be the best choice, fear of awarding an official, binding status to a relationship that might not be 'the right one' – as if, somewhere out there, the 'perfect' partner were waiting to make their lives complete. The truth is that there are millions of people of the other sex throughout the world with whom we could live happily ever after, provided we ourselves have the right attitude.

Many couples do not marry officially until a child is expected. In these cases they are marrying because of the child and not because they think that marriage is the best thing for them or that they are perfectly suited to each other. One argument for couples setting up home on a temporary, provisional basis is that it is easier to separate if they are not formally married, and sadly, they are right. The problem is that society, in an attempt to persuade couples to stay together, has made it difficult – and often painful and expensive – to obtain a divorce. Thus a lack of faith in the long-term prospects of marriage, coupled with the difficulties associated with divorce, may lead many couples to reject marriage in favour of living together. They are not in effect refusing marriage itself; they are expressing their dissatisfaction with the state of society and its laws.

CHOOSING WISELY

Here are a few points that can help us to choose a suitable partner. First of all, think carefully about marriage and make absolutely sure it is what you want. Marriage should be embarked on in a spirit of courage and optimism, not fear and resignation. Many girls marry out of fear of getting 'left on the shelf', or merely to get away from home and family, to gain what they call their 'independence', or even because they are tired of going out to work five days a week. It is true that with the emancipation of women such attitudes are not as common as they used to be, but they still exist.

Likewise, many men marry because they are tired of doing their own cooking and laundry and want someone to look after them. Or they covet an attractive woman in the same way they might covet a shiny new car: both are powerful status symbols. Men can be status symbols too: there are plenty of women who, although at heart unwilling to be dominated by their future mates, nevertheless seek the protection of 'a strong man', someone they can look up to.

Not only must you truly want to marry: that wish must be accompanied by faith. 'I believe I can make you happy' is the best basis for marriage. Marriages based on 'I hope you can make me happy' are most likely to be doomed to difficulty and disappointment. The important thing is for both partners to desire two things: true equality – equal worth as human beings with equal rights and responsibilities – and personal and mutual fulfilment.

As we noted in Chapter 1, this marriage of equals is something very new, something we have had little experience or tradition to prepare us for. One sign that old customs die hard is the way some European men go to the Philippines or Thailand to seek a wife; Americans do the same in Japan. They all hope to find there someone they can dominate, a submissive woman who knows nothing of western customs and will not expect to be treated as an equal. They find a woman who will be more of a slave than a modern wife, but after a few years her contact with western ways will teach her that she too has

59

certain rights, and she will begin to resent her role and the submissiveness will disappear.

To marry out of blind passion or in a fever of romantic infatuation is just as problematic as to marry for money or status. We are all bombarded with the whirlwind courtships and happy-ever-after endings so popular in today's books and films, but moonlight romance can look very different in the dispassionate light of day. Of course, mutual attraction draws people together, and there should be some kind of affection, but we should not expect some sort of 'great love' immediately. True love takes time, time to sow the seeds, time to tend them and time to let the flowers bloom and the fruit ripen naturally. A true and lasting love comes above all from joint effort and hard work: from weathering the storms together, working together, rearing children together and watching them grow. Choosing someone to share all this is a weighty matter, far too important to be left to a sudden whim or wave of passion.

It is right that physical appearance should have some influence on our choice of partners. It would be most unwise to marry someone whose physical appearance positively repelled you. But it is wise to steer clear of relationships based on physical attraction alone. Such relationships rarely stand the test of time, if only because our physical appearances change as time goes by. We use more dependable criteria even when merely choosing a pair of shoes: their appearance may be what first attracts us, but we also look for qualities that will wear well and suit our needs.

Finally, one of the most important factors in choosing a partner is to know oneself well, and to thoroughly investigate the character of our prospective partner. Only in this way can we assess the suitability of our choice and decide whether there is a good chance we can build a happy and peaceful partnership together. We will return to this point in the next chapter.

DO DIFFERENCES MATTER?

There will always be certain differences between two partners, whether they relate to lifestyle and personal taste such as sports and hobbies, or to bigger issues such as age, education, class, race, nationality or religion. Age differences deserve special consideration, although in theory, in a marriage of equals, they ought not to matter at all, and hopefully in the future they will not. A few years either way do not matter, but a woman who marries a man much younger than herself will certainly face social disapproval, especially when she is in her later years. Moreover, modern women mature faster than men of the same age, and the physical attraction of a younger man will soon cease to make up for his lack of maturity. And men who choose wives appreciably older than themselves may do so because of a lack of self-confidence, a fear of the other sex: they are looking for a mother rather than a mate.

On the other hand, society is more tolerant when an older man marries a much younger woman, although he may betray the desire to dominate a vulnerable girl or to acquire an attractive status symbol, and the young woman may be looking for a father-figure rather than a partner. As she matures and begins to expect greater equality in the relationship, friction can develop.

If we believe in social equality for everyone, including equality between the sexes, racial and cultural differences will seem unimportant to us. But we must never forget that marriage in itself demands a great deal of effort and co-operation if it is to produce a positive and lasting relationship. Racial and cultural differences obviously bring additional problems and stresses, and consequently it takes plenty of hard work from both partners in such a relationship if they are to achieve harmony, even when they seem ideally suited. That is why we usually advise against mixed marriages unless the people involved are fully aware of the problems ahead of them and are willing to face them together. The blending of races and cultures is in itself an excellent thing, a source of enrichment and vitality, but only if the couple face the difficulties that accompany mixed marriages and overcome them together. Both partners must enter the marriage with their eyes open, and take as their motto: 'We know it won't always be easy, but come what may we'll cope together.'

Major educational and social differences can still cause problems, especially when the wife is more highly educated than her husband or comes from a socially superior background. The last vestiges of masculine domination will take more than one generation to eradicate. The same goes for differences in income and financial status; when one partner comes from a particularly poor background and the other from an especially prosperous one, painful friction is almost inevitable, for each partner tends to hang onto the prejudices of his or her own social group.

Perhaps the reader will feel that not enough has been said here about shared tastes and interests, but the importance of this issue has often been overestimated. When people love and trust each other, a difference in interests does not much matter, and they can enjoy their favourite hobbies, or share their partners', without feeling uncomfortable either way. By taking an interest in someone else's hobbies we can learn something new as well as enjoying the pleasure of doing things together, but it is not necessary to do this all the time. The important thing is to understand that it is right and proper for each partner to have 'Lebensraum' – a space of one's own in which to live and breathe and develop. Without this personal space, even the most loving relationship can become a golden cage, and such restrictions are no good in the long run. A couple must be the sum of two complete personalities, not their lowest common denominator.

THREE IMPORTANT POINTS

Three points need to be thoroughly discussed before marriage: religion, child-rearing and the wife's career.

When partners do not share the same faith or the same church, it is important for them to decide from the start what attitude they are going to take towards religion. The woman must be aware that it will probably be more difficult for her to interest her future husband in her faith than vice versa. Too many men, unfortunately, still tend to attach insufficient importance to their wives' views on certain essential matters, and religion is one of them.

The question of children – whether to have children, if so when, how many and how they should be brought up – is the second area on which agreement should be sought in advance. The same goes for the children's academic and religious education. If one partner is a firm believer in the maintained school system and the other wants the children to be privately educated, it is better to discuss this before marriage.

Thirdly, and related to the second point, is the question of the wife's career. The day when the principle of equality between the sexes is completely incorporated into our social mores and put into practice in everyday life, will be the day when everyone will realize that the work of a mother and home-maker is the most important job in the country. A mother who makes and maintains a loving, welcoming home is creating an environment in which the whole family can grow and flourish, to everyone's benefit. In such an egalitarian society, spiritual values will come to the fore and purely economic and financial ones will take a back seat. Then many of today's 'impure motives' for having a professional occupation – such as for a woman to work outside the home merely to earn the money for a better car than the neighbours' – will hold less sway. Today, however, we are still living in a patriarchal society where materialism and competition set the pace.

Of course, for many couples in these days of high interest rates and a soaring cost of living, two incomes are not a luxury but a financial necessity, and the wives must have a career. Today's generation of young men have little difficulty in understanding that married women should have the opportunity for a career if they wish. It is not only the question of money or the issue of sexual equality; there are other advantages.

First of all, a working mother is not necessarily a bad mother, any more than a stay-at-home mother is necessarily a good one. The increasing importance and influence of women can only benefit society as a whole, and society should not need to wait until a woman's children have left home to benefit from her talents and training. The relationship between husband and wife will be enriched too, as both partners bring home the fruits of their experience and can bring them into their consultations together. Moreover women, as educators of the next generation, should ideally receive an education that is at least as good as if not better than men's, and as more women follow careers, girls' education and career training will be taken more seriously than in the past. This will benefit the children, as will the knowledge and experience of a professional mother, whilst a mother who is 'just a housewife' may lack the broad outlook and self-confidence that every good educator needs. The stay-at-home mother may also run the risk of feeling frustrated and trapped, and compensate for this by over-protecting her children. On the other hand, we all know many stay-at-home mothers who are supremely contented with their lot, and many working wives who would happily stay at home if only their financial circumstances permitted. It all boils down to finding a lifestyle that suits the whole family.

Several investigations have shown that, contrary to previous belief, separation from their mother has a positive effect on children. A mother who is always available on demand can stifle and spoil children instead of helping them to grow up. Of course, we are not talking about babies here: the mother's presence is almost indispensable in the first two years of life. But children whose mothers are absent from time to time become more independent, self-confident and resourceful. It is therefore worthwhile to arrange such separations occasionally, whether the mother uses this time to earn money, to attend classes or simply to relax and enjoy herself. The old maxim, 'look after the mother if you want to look after the child' is a valid one, since all too often in a marriage the woman is expected to care for husband and children, with little concern focused on her own needs. In the long run this is not in anyone's interests.

5

CAUSES OF CONFLICT

As a psychotherapist I have seen a great many couples in crisis. In all these troubled marriages their problems boil down to just four main causes. When both partners still wish to stay together and work at the marriage, an understanding of these four problem areas can aid reconciliation and even strengthen their unity as a couple. Indeed, anyone interested in their own development as a husband or wife, whether experiencing marital problems themselves or not, can still study these four causes of conflict and learn from them. Briefly, they are the urge to be right, our idle fancies and vain imaginings, our emotions, and our self-centredness.

THE URGE TO BE RIGHT

Every argument, big or small, starts with two people of opposing views, each equally convinced that he or she is right. If a person who is right insists on everyone acknowledging it, then he is putting himself in the wrong, for such stubborn insistence on having one's own way is a great enemy of both reason and justice, and a sure way of turning an insignificant disagreement into a major quarrel.

Of course we all have rights as well as responsibilities; but insisting on our own rights may mean disregarding the rights of others. There are times when, in the interests of harmony and equality, we are well advised not to insist on having the last word. Martin Luther once said:

> 'Peace is more valuable than being right. Peace was not made for the sake of right; right was made for the sake of peace. Therefore, if one should ever need to give way to the other, then right should give way to peace and not vice versa.'

And Robert Heinlein was only half joking when he advised couples, 'If you find you are in the right, apologize at once.'

Here is an example of the urge to be right, carried to extremes. A married couple come to the clinic. When the counsellor asks why they have come, the woman starts to explain. She has hardly opened her mouth, however, before her husband interrupts to correct her. Quickly she justifies herself. One thing leads to another and soon they are arguing fiercely. In the heat of battle both have forgotten the counsellor's existence. In their role as seasoned fighters for their rights they demonstrate their agreement – of which neither of them is conscious – to fight their battles with arguments.

Consultation

A different kind of agreement is needed to resolve the problems of the couple described above. The desire to be right, to justify and defend oneself and correct the other person will only prolong a quarrel. In a true discussion or consultation, such combative techniques have no place, and they prevent a couple from reaching any sort of conscious agreement on how they might extricate themselves from the situation and learn to live together in a spirit of unity.

So what could a couple in this situation do? Firstly, the question of who is right and who is wrong must be excluded from such discussions, because that always involves establishing one person's superiority over the other and such power struggles inevitably undermine a couple's sense of togetherness and unity. Of course, this does not mean giving up one's own point of view: nobody is obliged to subscribe to their partner's opinions, and everyone has a right to their own viewpoint. Indeed, we can't help but think differently, so differences are only to be expected, and we must learn to welcome them. Two heads are better than one, as they say, even if they differ: differing opinions can at least show us that nothing is as simple or as obvious as we think. Consequently, it is not necessary for a couple to be united in their every view. The unity that is important is that of having a united approach to the marriage and to solving problems together.

Keeping the lines of communication open is perhaps the most important aid to marital harmony. Emerson once said: 'The best of life is conversation, and the greatest success is confidence, or perfect understanding between sincere people.'⁸ Conversation or consultation at its best means co-operating, sharing thoughts, building a bridge between minds. It is perhaps the highest and most spiritual of all human relations. Conversation is an aid to thought. It enables us to put ourselves in the other person's place, to understand what makes him or her tick. But to make good conversation we need to adopt an optimistic approach, and to know how to listen attentively, then how to pursue a subject logically and systematically. Conversation is dependent on spirituality, and ideally entails our not demanding anything from the other person or wanting anything for ourselves, neither wishing to preach nor to assert our superiority. In short, it requires a balance between personal rights and self-sacrifice, and a spirit of true friendship.

Talking things over takes time, and should not be undertaken unless both partners are free to give it their whole attention. First of all the couple should agree on a suitable time for discussion. It is unreasonable to expect one's partner to be available at any time. Suppose a husband comes home one evening and wants to talk to his wife about something that happened at work. She is just getting their baby ready for bed. Impatient though he may be, the husband should realize that he must wait until his wife is free. Equally the wife should refrain from launching into a recital of her day's events – at home, in the office or wherever she works – before her husband has had the chance to unwind. Then, when the time is right and they can give each other their full attention, they can talk over the things that have been bothering them during the day.

Whatever they want to discuss, they should approach each other lovingly, gently and humbly: 'I need to talk something over with you; I could do with your advice. When would be a good time to talk?' Humility like this is also a form of courage. Humility is in woefully short supply today and we would do well to try to develop it. True humility never humiliated anyone because it emanates from self-control, inner strength and belief in oneself.

Apart from determining the time for discussion, it is also important to choose the right place. A true discussion cannot take place just anywhere. The best place is where we cannot be disturbed by the telephone, children or visitors. Why not go for a stroll together, or have coffee in a quiet café?

Having chosen the time and place to talk, there is a third condition: both partners must be in a reasonably good mood. If their hearts are not in it, they are hardly likely to consult well and achieve the agreement they are hoping for. And if, in the course of their conversation, the atmosphere becomes oppressive, or if one partner seems tired or impatient – all signs that the discussion has not been proceeding as it should have been – they must have the good sense to put off their discussion until later. It is a good idea to agree about this at the beginning, especially if the question to be discussed looks like being a contentious one. Both partners need to be in a good mood, or they will not be able to co-operate and stay focused on the facts, and nothing useful will come of their discussion.

The fourth and final condition for having a fruitful discussion is more difficult to satisfy: it is that your motives should be pure. Where there is absolute sincerity and goodwill, you will find mutual trust, and the discussion will proceed smoothly, neither side taking offence and both partners able to concentrate on the issues rather than on defending their own position.

For example, if you sincerely want your consultation to be constructive, you cannot afford to use it to further your own interests or to improve your position *vis-à-vis* your partner, however unconsciously. Common sense should tell you that if you try to score points off your partner by bringing up his problems, he will feel challenged or criticized, put down or accused – and will be so busy defending himself or planning revenge as to be unable to discuss the subject you raised in the first place. Nor is it enough to say, 'I've got a problem; I can't control the way I get angry every time you say or do such and such.' Despite your tactful opening, as long as your partner feels defensive he will see the remainder of your comments as an accusation, and over-react. The critical factor, therefore, is the purity of our motives for holding the discussion, and we must be honest about this with ourselves.

Reaching a mutually acceptable agreement on our future behaviour and the way forward for our relationship through discussion and consultation is only possible when both parties treat each other as equals. Successes like this then encourage us to persevere and try more of the same. Each successful discussion makes us realize that it is possible for a couple to live in peace and harmony, provided they regard each other as individuals with their own dignity and worth. Mutual respect and a sense of justice are the chief conditions for unity between husband and wife.

BUILDING CASTLES IN THE AIR

The second important cause of conflict is our abuse of that wonderful faculty, imagination. Imagination enhances our lives by supplementing the inadequacies of the real world, or our experience of it, and can also give us the vision to transform present reality into something new and better. As a creative faculty, imagination has a particularly exciting part to play in art and literature, invention and discovery. Imagination builds castles in the air in which children and the young at heart can dream their dreams in peace. We must not undervalue dreams, for they lead us to a wonderful world where everything is possible. But we must not forget to wake up from these dreams nor,

71

like Don Quixote and countless other dreamers, confuse dreams with reality.

So what is imagination? The power of imagination is a typically human function which, unlike the five outer senses we share with animals such as touch and sight, may be regarded as an inner sense. Our ability to think is our second inner sense, which we use to attain our third inner sense, our ability to understand. When we perceive something with our outer senses and want to understand it, we have first to imagine it before we can think about it.

If we imagine something, but are too lazy to think about it, instead of gaining understanding we develop prejudices. These are off-the-peg, second-hand opinions that are the product of accepting the judgements that result from other people's thinking without first examining them ourselves and weighing them in the balance of our own understanding. Such second-hand, impersonal thinking may come from friends or family or from books, newspapers, radio, television or even from education and other sources.

Throughout its long history, the human race has always had a tendency to build up a body of settled opinion clad in the robes of universally received tradition. These are usually flattering when applied to ourselves, derogatory when applied to others: other races, other social or religious groups, other customs. We embrace these prejudices because we find them comforting, or because we are too lazy to form independent opinions of our own, or because they flatter the good opinion we like to have of ourselves.

What has all this to do with marital problems? A great deal. Many couples live together for years, fondly believing they know all about each other and in reality ignorant of everything except a paltry collection of ideas, opinions and misconceptions that each has built up about the other on the flimsiest of evidence. One day, when your imagination is off duty, you may open your eyes and be unpleasantly surprised to find you have been living with a stranger all these years. Perhaps you have heard the story of the couple on their Golden Wedding day.

'Unselfishness is what marriage is all about,' said Mike. 'For fifty years I've been eating chicken legs because I knew you preferred the breast.'

'But I don't,' said Joan. 'I prefer the leg, but I always gave it to you because I thought it was your favourite.'

Touching though it is, that story illustrates how little many couples really tell each other. Yet if we have not even discussed such simple matters as eating preferences, think how much harder it is to share our ideas about more important subjects like our relationship and marriage itself.

Know each other

As we noted in the last chapter, it is very important that we really get to know well our prospective partner before marriage, so that we do not marry a figment of our imagination. The worst situation is when one partner only loves the image he or she has built up of the other and does not actually love the other person for him or herself. Such marriages seldom last.

Marriage is a melting-pot in which two separate people become one couple without losing their individuality. Becoming a couple involves revealing things about yourself while at the same time discovering things about your partner. Where this process of shared intimacy does not take place, it is very hard to achieve this closeness and form a true partnership. Basically, then, many marriages founder because partners do not really know and understand each other. They build up a picture of their partner in their imaginations and then complain when the living, breathing person does not conform to those specifications. Or perhaps one partner changes and develops over the years, and the other does not notice. The person you married ten years ago has not stood still, and neither have you. It is vital, therefore, to spend time getting to know one's partner – and this must be an ongoing process. Couples can never know each other too thoroughly, and the best way to get to know one's partner is through frank discussion and sharing one's innermost thoughts and feelings.

OUR EMOTIONS AND FEELINGS

In discussing the third cause of conflict, we must first make a clear distinction between positive and negative emotions or feelings. In Adlerian philosophy, emotions are described as negative feelings, and are regarded as negative in the sense that they are socially disruptive, degrading us and harming others. Feelings, on the other hand, may be described as positive emotions. They are socially constructive and benefit both ourselves and others. Destructive emotions make living together a negative experience, while positive feelings are joyful and uplifting and their highest expression is love – real love, and not what is often understood by the word today. Love within the microcosm of a couple is the first step towards universal, spiritual love. Theologians sometimes speak of four kinds of love.

First, on the highest level, is the love God has for Himself. Human beings will never be able to understand this love. Then comes God's love for us. This love is the source of all the love in creation. Our love for God is the third type of love; this is the origin of our love for our fellow 'men', for humankind. We are not, however, able to love all people impartially, for their own sakes, without the help of God, who created us all and loves us all equally. The fourth form of love is the love that human beings have for each other. This love, however, can be described as true, spiritual love only if we remember to include God in the relationship.

St Paul says, 'There is nothing love cannot face; there is no limit to its faith, its hope, and its endurance.'[9] Love like this does not come automatically. We have to learn it, like walking and speaking. It comes from selflessness, trust and respect. As Rudolf Dreikurs, a leading Adlerian counsellor, noted, love is 'the means for the greatest contribution to another person, the surrender of everything that one has and is, the most upright expression of the longing to belong'. Yet why is this true, pure love so much rarer than our negative emotions? Bahá'u'lláh provides an answer: 'Love is a light that never dwelleth in a heart possessed by fear'.[10] True love requires courage, and we live in a discouraging world.

Negative emotions are the personal, poisonous, self-centred feelings that have their roots in a sense of inferiority; they represent an impulsive reaction, an exaggerated response, to a person's environment. Animals feel such emotions too, whereas only human beings are capable of the true spiritual love that is God's gift to humankind. Emotional people react immediately in an impulsive, primitive way because they are not confident of being able to achieve their aim with any other means at their disposal. Most people are reluctant to believe this, because being emotional and giving easy vent to one's feelings is fashionable nowadays; the majority of modern novels, plays and films lay great emphasis on the impulsive expression of emotions. It is important to differentiate here between impulsiveness and spontaneity: impulsiveness is self-centred, negative and brings conflict, whereas spontaneity is outgoing, positive and brings harmony. Our reluctance to curb our impulsiveness is easily explained, because it provides an excellent excuse for destructive and antisocial behaviour. But we must make such distinctions and learn to control our emotions if we want to become more human and to live in a gentler, more peaceful world.

Control those emotions

There is a way of controlling destructive emotions. First, we must learn to develop a positive attitude. There is nothing that cannot be regarded in a positive light if we so decide; this was discussed in Chapter 3. With practice we can become not only more impartial but more optimistic. A positive view enables us to judge each situation on its merits – we can stand back from a problem and take the broad, objective view. We can lay aside our self-centred attitudes and become more other-centred, more socially aware, and develop greater courage. This helps us to progress from merely reacting, animal-like, to a situation, to acting. In other words, we can learn to be in control of ourselves rather than being controlled by others, and so attain true freedom through self-control.

In taking a positive view it is helpful to learn to distinguish between people and things, between the deed and the doer. Jesus told us to hate the sin while continuing to love the sinner. Whatever a person has said or done to offend us, we should still value that person as a fellow human being and thereby accept his or her weaknesses and mistakes. In other words, we can reject the behaviour, but not the person. Nobody is perfect, and it is only when we have learned to distinguish between the person and his or her behaviour that we can truly love our neighbour –

as we would wish to be loved, despite our shortcomings, ourselves. It is perfectly possible, moreover, that the person who has offended us may turn over a new leaf: if we are wise, we will wait patiently for this to happen, without ourselves closing any possible channels of communication by acting on impulse. It is also possible that we have misunderstood a person or situation, and separating the deed and doer protects the relationship and allows problems to be sorted out in time. Many people suffer through their own ignorance; we must educate them. Others are like children and need to be guided towards maturity. It is our responsibility to help and teach in this way, but in doing so we must beware of feeling superior. Good deeds done in a spirit of condescension and self-satisfaction are not good at all.

This positive attitude is optimistic as well as benevolent, because positive people are hopeful people who look on the bright side of life. Pessimism, on the other hand, by its focus on the negative, sets up a vicious circle: believing that something bad will happen is the surest way of seeing that it comes about. People who live in dread of failure, illness or misfortune are the most likely to fail, fall ill or suffer hardships. Many rationalize their pessimism by saying, 'If I am a pessimist, I can never be disappointed; in fact, I will be only too pleased to be proved right. And if by chance something good happens, then I won't be disappointed to be proved wrong but will simply enjoy it more.'

An optimist, on the other hand, experiences greater happiness and approaches life with more courage, his efforts unhindered by fear of failure or misfortune. Moreover, he has already seen through the psychological trick of deciding not to feel disappointed, and has at his disposal other tools than the pessimist's one of having to be right.

Optimism, then, is not only more appropriate – it is a necessity if we are to develop our true potential and lead a full and productive life. Since there are no negative forces actively working against us, the future will be whatever our own courage and intelligence, resourcefulness and faith can make of it.

Although it is still customary in our society to magnify our good deeds and to hide our bad deeds, the true optimist does exactly the opposite. When he has done something good, he tries to conceal it, because to him it is the deed that counts, not recognition by others, which he in actual fact already has. We read in the Bible that he who fasts, gives alms and prays so that others notice and praise him as a pious man 'has had his reward'; but if I keep my good deed to myself, I become more and more 'good', that is, more positive and more able to do good. In other words, good deeds performed in secret are credited to our account in 'heaven'; good deeds that receive praise on earth have little value in the next life. It is as if I took money to the bank and my savings grew and grew and produced interest: 'a person is what he keeps'. Consequently, we must live our lives to the best of our ability, not expecting acclaim or reward.

Likewise, if we humbly admit our mistakes, our debts in heaven will be cancelled and we can start again with a clean slate. The optimist, for example, admits his mistakes both to God and to himself – and, depending on the situation, also to others, but not in a way that would be humiliating to him. He lets the negative, the bad, out, and does not keep it like a debt. In this way he has no debts to the bank, or at least, does not increase them, while the pessimist who keeps his mistakes to himself finds that his debts increase continuously and he becomes more and more negative, because, as we have already said, a

78

person is what he keeps. However, he does let people know of his good deeds, and thus gives out his good things immediately and has no positive savings. Just like the optimist, he is right in the way he sees things, which is very important for him. But what he does not know is that with his negative attitude, he attracts negative things to himself.

One way of freeing ourselves from the slavery of our emotions and becoming masters of our feelings is to use our knowledge of the five short-term goals discussed in Chapter 3. We must never forget that a peaceful, harmonious and fruitful relationship with another person depends not on *avoiding* situations likely to lead to dispute or confrontation but on confronting them in a positive, understanding and helpful spirit. Nothing can be achieved through violence and arguments – except more violence and arguments. Neither should we give in for the sake of preserving the peace, since giving in is just as bad as arguing. When I argue with someone, I insult his or her dignity, and in giving in I insult my own. The answer must be based on mutual respect. There is a phrase that we can apply to this situation that will help us live together in peace: 'Neither argue nor give in but understand and want to help'.

If I repress my emotions, control myself and curb my tongue, I am fighting myself. However, fighting can never be right. But if I give way to my emotions, give them free rein, then I hurt others and make a difficult situation worse, which cannot be right either. Furthermore, I would then be following the pleasure principle that reigns today, where I simply let myself go and do only what I want to do, regardless of the consequences for others. The result of the pleasure principle, which is not generally known, is that my unwillingness to do what is right grows and I make less and less effort.

The answer is to find a solution where there are no winners *or* losers, where the only aim is to try to understand and help each other. This is where the unconscious short-term goals we discussed earlier come in. Let us briefly list those goals again. They are: seeking an excuse, seeking attention, the desire to assert one's superiority, desire for revenge, and the urge to withdraw and sulk. 'Know yourself,' said Plato. Montaigne said the same many centuries later. When we know ourselves and learn to recognize the goals motivating our behaviour, those fits of raw emotion will become less frequent, less intense and of shorter duration. While we are getting to know ourselves, the need to understand will absorb and channel our energy, claim our attention and distract us from those emotions that were only threatening to us when they were out of our control. Moreover, once we have gained some understanding of our own motives, we can begin to understand the goals our partner is pursuing with his or her behaviour, which will help us learn to react less and to focus instead on how we can really help.

This is the first step towards the flowering of the only really positive feeling there is. Every peaceful human relationship is based on it. Marital understanding depends on it. It is true, spiritual love, and spiritual love means listening to one's partner, paying attention, taking an interest and treating one's partner with respect. By loving our partner, we acknowledge that he or she is as close and precious to us as ourselves, and we will find it much easier to live together in peace.

SELF-CENTREDNESS

The fourth cause of conflict is self-centredness; of all human failings, it is the hardest to overcome. It is also, unfortunately, the one that poses the greatest threat to marital unity. Self-centredness stems from a feeling of inferiority, a lack of faith and self-confidence, and from discouragement. Self-centred people are timid people; the less courage we have, the more self-centred we are. The less we feel able to face the trials of life, the more we curl up like hedgehogs, presenting only our prickles to the outside world.

Self-centredness should not be confused with selfishness. Of course, selfish people are always self-centred, but not all self-centred people are selfish. Self-centred people can learn to hide their fears from other people and from themselves, and even strike a bold posture on occasion. Inside, however, self-centred people are deeply unhappy because they do not trust anyone, and have no confidence in themselves, in their own bodies, in the world around them or even in life itself. It follows that they do not believe in success, any more than they believe in their own feelings or abilities, and that they are extremely vulnerable. They would like to be independent, but are afraid of the responsibilities that freedom brings. What is more, without realizing it, self-centred people make themselves dependent on everything and everybody: on science, medicine, psychology, society. To escape their misery they may seek short-term satisfaction in tobacco, alcohol or other drugs.

Self-mastery

The spiritual path. The most important way in which we can master self-centredness is by taking a more spiritual path in life, since this is the path that will take us from self to spirituality. Rather than go into detail about what is and is not meant by spirituality, let me give some examples of self-centred and spiritual behaviour:

The self-centred person is a slave to his emotions; the spiritual person is their master.

The self-centred person measures everything and everyone on a 'superior/inferior' scale; the spiritual person's yardsticks are God's will and the general good.

The self-centred person looks back to the past; the spiritual person lives in the present and looks boldly towards the future.

The self-centred person is preoccupied with causes; the spiritual person sets goals.

The self-centred person is anxious to be proved right; the spiritual person wants only to live at peace with everyone.

The self-centred person criticizes other people; the spiritual person is content simply to love them.

The self-centred person focuses on other people's mistakes and delights in judging them; the spiritual person has eyes only for their good qualities, and differentiates between people and their deeds.

The self-centred person gets angry with people; the spiritual person wants to help them.

The self-centred person broadcasts his good deeds and carefully conceals his mistakes; the spiritual person broadcasts his mistakes and hides his good deeds.

The self-centred person is motivated by the five short-term, socially disturbing goals; the spiritual person desires harmony and a closer relationship with God.

The self-centred person draws his strength from misuse of human and natural resources; the spiritual person draws his strength from the word of God.

The self-centred person is a pessimist; the spiritual person is an optimist.

The self-centred person's life is in turmoil; the spiritual person's life is orderly and planned.

The self-centred person lives in doubt; the spiritual person lives in faith.

The self-centred person is always saying, 'Something should be done!'; the spiritual person asks himself, 'What can I do to help?'

Unconsciously, the self-centred person makes himself dependent on everyone and everything; the spiritual person enjoys inner freedom.

'Oh dear, that's difficult!' says the self-centred person; 'What a wonderful challenge!' says the spiritual person.

It is clear that what we should strive for on the spiritual path is self-forgetfulness, and self-forgetfulness comes from being drawn out of ourselves by love: love of a beloved person, love of all that is beautiful and good, love of everything that is holy.

The first and most decisive step towards self-forgetfulness is prayer. When we turn towards God we turn towards the supreme good, and as our thoughts turn to Him, so our feelings – and actions – will follow. Thus we can gradually spiritualize our lives through prayer, meditation, and the study and practical application of the teachings of the major religions, for of course prayer and meditation are not tied to any particular religious tradition. God understands us all.

Real prayer does not mean asking God to make our wishes come true, but asking Him to help us conform our wishes to His will. This is the only way to the peace and inner contentment that prayer can give. And prayer must be accompanied by deeds.

'Prayer and meditation are very important factors in deepening the spiritual life of the individual, but with them must go also action and example, as these are the tangible result of the former. Both are essential.'[11]

Do not compare yourself. We have seen that the first step we can take towards mastering self-centredness is to embark on a more spiritual path. Let us now go one step further. For this we must practice not comparing ourselves with others. Let us lay aside all this obsessive self-examination, all this preoccupation with our own weaknesses, this compulsion to compare ourselves with other people all the time: 'Am I doing all right? Am I better or worse than them?' A self-centred person continually thinks about himself and tries to assess himself *vis-à-vis* others; this anxious self-examination is uncomfortably tied up with, 'What do other people think of me? What sort of impression am I making? Will they appreciate my true worth? Do they accept me or do they think I'm stupid?' These are the questions that haunt so many people today, but they are the concerns of a self-centred person.

In comparing ourselves with another person, we invariably make the mistake of using as a yardstick our different talents and skills in order to measure our comparative value and worth. Yes, of course we can compare talents, abilities and so on, but we cannot compare *people*. Every human being, with his or her own distinct spiritual and psychological make-up, is totally unique and therefore incomparable. Thus the temptation to compare people with one another contradicts the principle of equality towards which, willingly or otherwise, our society is moving. Moreover, if we compare ourselves with others in order to establish a sense of superiority and bolster our own ego, this is bound to interfere with our relationships.

Do not take yourself too seriously. Another step towards our goal of self-forgetfulness is to decide not to take ourselves too seriously. We have seen how the surges of uncontrolled feeling that we call our emotions are harmful and that peace depends on attaching less importance to them and so freeing ourselves from them. But this does not mean fighting them. The self-centred, emotional, animal side of ourselves that threatens to take over our lives must be trained by kindness, not beaten into submission. Let us call it our ego. The point is that our small ego is not only negative. We simply have to handle it properly and not let it dominate our lives like a ham actor always hogging the limelight. We should speak gently to it, as to a well-trained dog: 'I'm busy just now, Ego. Go and lie down. I'll take you for a walk when I've got time.' Remembering to do this every now and then is a good way of learning to forget our ego.

Having trained our ego to take a back seat, we are in a better position to look dispassionately at our emotions and our selfish preoccupations, and even to be amused by them. Our ego is like a family pet: it lives with us but does not rule the roost. Once we have learned to be detached from our ego and no longer regard it as being so important, we can learn to laugh at ourselves, which is a sign that we are on the right road: the spiritual path. We have begun to live the conscious, spiritual life; we have broken the vicious circle of self-absorption.

Of course, we shall never banish our ego altogether: that would imply perfection, of which no human being is capable. What we can hope for is spiritual progress, which brings our ego increasingly under the control of our enlightened, spiritual side.

Be detached from success and failure. A further step towards self-mastery is the realization that success, like failure, does not tell us much about a person. If we have failed today, that does not mean we shall not succeed tomorrow. Success is primarily a matter of perseverance and does not depend only on us. The important thing is to try our best. As Kipling said, 'If you can meet with Triumph and Disaster/And treat those two impostors just the same'[12] you have the right idea.

We must resist the temptation to blame our failures on bad luck or circumstances beyond our control. We must battle on, our eyes fixed on the finishing line, which we are sure of reaching eventually – provided, of course, that the goal we are pursuing is a real one and not a mirage. In this way we can save ourselves the trouble of making excuses for our mistakes or – even worse – blaming them on other people.

In our struggles for self-mastery we should remember that the prophets themselves were not spared these struggles. They too experienced pain, illness and suffering, but triumphed over them by sheer spiritual strength. When trouble overwhelms us we should try to do the same. The sufferings of this world are transitory: we shall win through in the end.

The power of belief. Self-centredness, as we have seen, is characterized by an inability to believe in ourselves: the more we doubt ourselves, the more self-absorbed we become and the more seriously we take ourselves. On the other hand, the more we come to believe in ourselves, the less seriously we take ourselves. However, even where we believe in ourselves, it is usually in only one aspect of ourselves that we have especially trained and developed. Successful business people, for example, may believe that they can be successful in their careers while having little faith that they can be successful lovers or fathers. Conversely, some men are wonderful fathers and friends, but are hopeless at making money. Of course, they could be successful in business if they believed in themselves more, since the power of belief can be very strong.

Let us take the example of an extremely pretty young woman who is firmly convinced that she is plain. Where, you may ask, does her conviction come from? Perhaps in her childhood she was in competition with a very pretty sister, and so came to believe she was an ugly duckling. Such is the power of her belief that neither the mirror nor the protestations of those around her can persuade her to the contrary.

Similarly, a great many young men nowadays build up an imaginary picture of what a 'real' man must be like, and yet do not believe that they can ever live up to this ideal. The consequences can be dramatic – inferiority complexes, inhibitions, shyness, introversion, anxiety, fear of the opposite sex – and can lead to difficulties in forming relationships with the other sex, homosexuality or even suicide. In fact, the belief is then justified by the outcome, and we have what is called a self-fulfilling prophecy.

The power of belief has become widely accepted through the use of placebos in medicine. Placebos, of course, are harmless substances that in theory can have no effect on the body. And yet the vast majority of patients who are given placebos by doctors whom they trust will insist that the medicine is doing them good. The more the doctor praises the medicine, the more good it does the patient. It is obvious, then, that the effect of the placebo is psychological, not physiological; the patient's belief that the placebo will help has cured him.

We all need to believe in order to live. Belief is the only thing in this world that gives us a feeling of certainty; when we believe, we are sure about what we are doing. It does not matter what we believe in – we can believe in our church as much as we believe in our political party. We believe in an idea as much as in our family, our partners, our children or in life itself. People can be induced to believe in practically anything. History is scattered with fallen idols who led whole civilizations astray. A glance at recent history is enough to show us what monstrous heresies this power of belief can give rise to.

It is also easy to understand why Faith with a capital 'F' is so widely mistrusted. Whatever we may understand by Faith, examples of its misuse are legion: the media are full of it. Many fine minds, therefore, take refuge in scepticism, doubt and debate, which has resulted in the enfeeblement of the major traditional religious institutions. Moreover, since the need to believe in something is as essential to humanity as fresh air and food, this need, if it is not satisfied, tends to manifest itself in a proliferation of 'psi' beliefs, a sickness of the soul that is so widespread nobody is safe from it. One of the greatest problems today is that our society is going through a great crisis of Faith. I repeat, we all need to believe in something – but in what?

One man was assisted along his path to faith by the realization that all the really great men of history and of the sciences – at least towards the end of their lives – had some kind of religious belief, though cynics might interpret this as a sign of senility rather than wisdom! But today, too, it is the great physicists and biologists who realize that behind all things there must be a spiritual principle unifying the natural forces they have studied all their lives. Ordinary people have known about this spiritual force for thousands of years; they call it God.

Some years ago the celebrated physicist Max Planck announced that matter in itself does not exist, and that the various laws of physics to which matter was subject were drawn up, not by chance but on purpose, by a conscious, intelligent spirit greater than our own. He said:

'This spirit is the cause and origin of all material things. Reality is not the things which are visible: these are in fact ephemeral. What is real, what IS, is this invisible, eternal spirit. Only He exists! That is why I am not afraid to call this mysterious creator by the name which all nations and cultures have called Him through the ages, for thousands of years: God!'[13]

Human beings have a huge capacity for belief, whether in God, in ourselves or in some philosophy or ideal. So how can we learn to really believe? The conscious decision to concentrate on the *positive* in life, in other people and in oneself, can be a great help. There is nothing in my inner life or in the world around me that I cannot regard positively in some way.

An additional, conscious aid is the recognition that, as we have seen, belief is a function that we use all the time, unconsciously or not. We must also recognize that fear is a form of negative belief, and whether positive or negative, belief has an effect. Thus if we believe we are going to succeed in some enterprise or if we believe in a spiritual goal, we are half-way there already, and conversely, those who fear their own inadequacy will usually become inadequate.

So in our marriages, we must try not only to believe in ourselves and become less self-centred, but also to believe in our partners more and so help them to believe in themselves. And, of course, we must believe in the relationship and have faith in the future, for without this we will not invest as much in the marriage and – as we have seen – it will be much more likely to fail.

6

CONFLICT-SOLVING

CREATING UNITY

In the last chapter we looked at various causes of conflict and a sense of separation, and we described key factors that when applied to problems of disunity can lead to the syndrome of togetherness, even unity. Here is a simple table showing this process at work:

From the separation syndrome:	by using:	to a state of:	to the unity syndrome:
being right	discussion, consultation	agreement	justice
ideas	discussion	certainty	insight
emotions	5 short-term goals and a positive attitude	more positive feelings	love
self-centredness	spiritualization	spirituality	belief

The four factors of the unity syndrome, justice, insight, love and belief, all have as their standard: 'Let deeds, not words, be your adorning'.[14] Each of us can use them on a daily basis to see just how far we have come in our spiritual development. For example, we can ask ourselves, 'To what degree am I just in my behaviour? Do I live my life in accordance with my new insight – am I putting this new knowledge into practice? Do I show my love in my deeds? Do I make others happy? Do I serve them? Do I feel responsible for other people and do I help them to believe in themselves more?'

If we try to follow the path from self-centredness to spirituality, from wanting to always be in the right and to feel superior to justice, from building castles in the air to understanding reality, and from allowing our emotions free rein to developing the courage and selflessness to experience true love – if we progress along this path to unity, we will find ourselves better prepared to live with our partners in peace and harmony, and in a better position to resolve our differences and solve our conflicts.

FIVE BASIC RULES

There are five simple rules for resolving differences and avoiding conflict. Following these rules enables couples to extricate themselves painlessly from potentially contentious situations, handle conflicts better and thereby increase their confidence in the relationship.

Rule 1: Be positive

Accept the situation as it is, which means acknowledging the problem but resisting any impulse to run away from it. The mere fact that we have accepted a situation, however unpleasant, puts us in a more favourable position to overcome it. Life is full of hurdles and every one we clear makes us stronger and better people. We can choose to look on every problem as an insurmountable obstacle that we must try to avoid, but this only deepens our lack of belief in ourselves and forces us to make endless excuses for our behaviour. Or we can acknowledge the problem and accept it as yet another challenge, as a potential blessing in disguise. At the very least, such a positive attitude will encourage us and strengthen our resolve, our self-confidence and our faith.

We should not expect to be able to solve everything, or to see results immediately. Nor do we need to react to failure by developing feelings of disappointment or dissatisfaction with ourselves. As we have seen, our mood depends entirely on ourselves and our own choices. Sweep away all discouraging feelings of impotence; banish 'difficult' and 'impossible' from your vocabulary, and even from your thoughts – simply using these words in relation to problems has a crippling effect, and you find yourself in a vicious circle. The more you use them, the harder it is to act effectively, and the more difficult and insurmountable the problem will seem – which in turn will discourage you further. However, it is easy enough to decide not to let such words pass your lips: banish them from your mind too, for all too often their main purpose is to provide a handy excuse in case of failure.

The important thing is to look at difficulties in a positive light. The great psychologist Alfred Adler advises us to believe in perfection, yet have the courage to be imperfect. Even though perfection is unattainable, we must nevertheless strive for it constantly. Perfection should be our aim; however, we are only human and it is natural for us to have human failings and shortcomings. The important thing is not to avoid making mistakes, but rather to try to turn large ones into less serious ones.

Finally, it is important to realize that potential conflicts and arguments cannot be resolved by words alone. You must carry your positive attitude over into your actions. You need to do the right thing too, some loving action that will reach your partner's heart, relieve tension, re-establish confidence and disarm aggression.

Rule 2: Respect your partner

A healthy, harmonious relationship is impossible without mutual respect, because respect is essential to true equality. An important prerequisite for respecting others is always to take care to distinguish between the subject of dispute and the person who is involved. As noted in Chapter 5, we must learn to reject the deed but never the doer. Obviously, if my beloved wife has said or done something which hurts me deeply, it is perfectly reasonable for me to resent her behaviour. What would be unreasonable would be for me to allow her *behaviour* to call into question all the love and respect I bear for *her*. Rejecting her as a person on this basis would not only be illogical, it would also adversely affect the peace and harmony of our relationship. We must learn to love our fellow human beings in spite of their weaknesses – just as we would wish to be loved ourselves. As Jesus said, 'He that is without sin among you, let him first cast a stone.'[15] Predictably, nobody threw any stones on that occasion. We are not saints, but merely fallible human beings ourselves, and we must therefore be prepared to excuse other people's failings and continue to love and respect them. Once we have learnt to distinguish between the doer and the deed, it will be easier and easier to love our partners – in spite of what they may have said or done.

Mutual respect also entails neither arguing nor giving way, but trying instead to understand and help. That is the attitude to take if you wish to live at peace with your partner – not like the parents in the old story:

'Haven't you got a daddy?'
'No.'
'Who does your mummy fight with, then?'

If only because we know that argument only leads to more argument, we should consciously avoid this 'method' of resolving a dispute. In fact, we should not only avoid the open 'hot' war of angry disputes and shouting matches, but also resist the urge to stir the embers of conflict beneath the surface of the relationship, the 'cold' war of verbal duels, innuendos and fine barbs designed to hurt. Both 'hot' and 'cold' warfare perpetuate a state of conflict and undermine the relationship. Giving in is no resolution at all because, as we discussed in the last chapter, it insults my own worth, but in quarrelling I insult my partner's worth. The only way to retain mutual respect and move from a situation of conflict to one of harmony is to avoid arguing as much as possible, and to resolve your conflicts by trying to understand and help.

Rule 3: Put yourself in the other person's place

Wanting to help is the first step, but we cannot be effective until we have really understood how the disagreement came about, and the part each protagonist played in causing it. To do this, we need empathy: the ability to put ourselves in the other person's place and see the situation through his or her eyes.

We can only really help if we put aside that urge to be right at all costs discussed in Chapter 5 and avoid criticizing and blaming our partner. Reproaches and recriminations only serve to put the other person down and since no one likes being at a disadvantage, our partner will be unwilling to accept this and will obviously try to defend himself. He may even try to reverse the situation with counter-accusations. We live in an age of discouragement and, as a result, instead of simply concerning ourselves with redressing a situation and re-establishing our equality, we have learned to over-compensate, to want to be superior. In a confrontational situation, we tend to react to a put-down by feeling the need to justify ourselves so strongly that we feel superior to our partner – but this places him at a disadvantage, a vicious circle is set up and the conflict escalates.

Disagreement causes us pain, but we must never lose sight of the pain the other person is feeling. In our self-centredness we often imagine that we carry the woes of the world on our shoulders, but we are mistaken; other people suffer too, whether they acknowledge this openly or not.

We must also remember how we ourselves feel about unsolicited advice, and avoid doling it out too readily. We all spent most of our youth being advised and admonished by our parents and teachers, and as adults we resent being told what and what not to do. In a conflict situation it is particularly unhelpful to tell the other person what he should or should not do – it will only serve to annoy him even more.

Finally, we must avoid focusing on our partner's short-comings and mistakes. That is the surest way of stirring up trouble. People who constantly bewail the faults and errors of others are trying to gain a feeling of superiority at their expense. We all make mistakes: that is what makes us human. As Goethe noted, 'Man must strive, and striving he must err',[16] and Pope said, 'To err is human, to forgive divine.'[17]

Rule 4: Understand the real reasons for the conflict

If we fail to look beyond the apparent causes of a dispute, we are like the gardener who thinks he is controlling the weeds by pulling off their leaves. All good gardeners know that the way to eradicate weeds is to tear them up by the roots. It is the same with disagreements: we have to look for the problems under the surface. Beneath every obvious cause for dispute there is always some underlying source of tension, usually attributable to one of the five short-term goals outlined in Chapter 3.

We need to recognize and take into account not only the other person's short-term goal but our own. This makes it easier to deal with the negative emotions that conflict arouses in us. We must never forget that we ourselves are answerable for our own emotions and therefore responsible for our anger and all our other negative and socially disturbing feelings. How can I blame my partner when only I can create such emotions in myself? We need to consider each of the short-term goals, therefore, until we find out which one we are pursuing with this behaviour. Then, when we have found the root of the problem, we can deal with it at once.

Rule 5: Reach an agreement

If two people are drawn up in battle array, that is because they have agreed, unconsciously, to do battle, to argue with each other. What we should be aiming for, however, is conscious communication. Leave the battlefield; only battles take place on battlefields. Sit down at the table with a pot of tea, and talk. Try to change your unconscious mutual agreement – to argue – and work towards conscious mutual agreement – for peace.

Couples owe it to themselves always to share each other's difficulties. Each and every problem should be regarded as a shared problem. Never say to your partner, 'That's your problem.' That is a thoroughly unsympathetic and uncaring reply. Of course there may be difficulties that concern only one partner, but each should be concerned about the other's problems, without attempting to sort them out for him. It goes without saying that it is only natural to want to help someone you love to solve his problems; he should be able to count on your listening ear, on your point of view, on your thoughtful and effective help.

To reach an agreement, you must be able to bury the past and refer to it only to learn from it. We cannot change the past, so we should forget it and channel our efforts into the present. So-called facts usually belong to the past, and trying to ascertain the facts often means endlessly raking over the past: 'What did he say? What did the other person do?' Leave such inquests to the lawyers. However important facts may be for them, two people who love each other must not poison their relationship like this; the only thing that matters about facts is what use we decide to make of them. Are we going to torture ourselves with reminders of yesterday's mistakes, or use them to learn how to live more harmoniously together? That is what needs agreement. Conflicts and disharmony can best be smoothed away by each of us deciding to forget the past and devoting our energies to the creation of a constructive future.

Every disagreement concerns both partners, and reaching an agreement therefore requires better co-operation and sharing of responsibilities. 'What can I change about myself? What should *I* do?' are the questions we should be asking ourselves. 'What should he (or she) do?' leads us into a minefield: away from co-operating and towards commanding and requiring. The first, indispensable step towards co-operation and sharing responsibility is to consult together, to talk things over in a friendly, open-minded way, followed by planning the next step together. We must always do so in a positive spirit of confidence, that is to say, the tireless optimism of two people in love.

These five recommendations are useful not only for overcoming marital difficulties, but for all kinds of conflict. Of course, many other approaches to conflict-solving are conceivable; but these have stood the test of time. They are certain to work, provided you make up your mind to have faith in them.

THE PHYSICAL SIDE

It is a universally acknowledged fact that sex plays a considerable role in the life of modern-day couples. Sexuality is a marvellous, God-given gift. Sexual pleasure is one of the natural rights of every human being, and it was with this in mind that the institution of marriage was created. It is, however, as reprehensible to overemphasize it as to play it down.

One young couple faced an all-too-common problem: the husband wanted sexual relations more frequently than the wife did. She would often have been content with his physical nearness and a cuddle. At first she forced herself to comply with his wishes, hoping that in time she would come to want it as much as he did; however, she found instead that sexual intercourse became more and more of an ordeal. She became increasingly convinced that her husband was literally using her. She tried all sorts of excuses to avoid it: one day she had a headache, the next day something important to do in the kitchen. But her conscience was troubling her. Her husband, who was of course most unhappy about all this, was wondering what he could possibly have done wrong. They quarrelled, and he accused his wife of frigidity. The two of them became more and more discouraged. Eventually they read a book together, which prompted them to seek psychiatric help. As they still loved each other, they hoped to solve their problems together.

A problem of this kind is not chiefly a sexual one. To overcome what seems a physical difficulty, we must know and understand the influences that have affected and are affecting both partners. Only then are we in a position to understand what each partner can do to put their sexual relations on the right lines again – without allowing their sexuality to dominate their lives.

In the past, man dominated woman and took it upon himself to take the initiative in sexual matters. Today, society is working towards equality between men and women in sexual matters as in everything else. Nevertheless, we are still living in a male-dominated society in which men are desperately trying to safeguard their ancient privileges and women are, justifiably, trying equally desperately to fight their way out of their inferior position. In this undeclared 'war', sexuality takes on the character of a 'weapon'. Neither partner is prepared to allow the other to call the tune.

It is still fashionable to believe there are mental, temperamental and emotional differences between men and women as well as straightforward sexual ones. This is a prejudice inherited from times past and is the result of a long tradition of male dominance. On a temperamental level, as on a spiritual one, these differences will tend to disappear as acceptance of equal rights and responsibilities between the sexes becomes more general. As noted in Chapter 1, social custom lags behind legislation in matters of equality between the sexes and practice has not yet caught up with theory. Meanwhile, it is vital for couples to tell each other what they need. In this, as in all other matters, couples need to set up a dialogue.

It is obvious that the couple described above have much to learn with each other as well as from each other. The husband must recognize that he would be just as wrong to demand sex from his wife whenever he wishes, as he would be to worry excessively about the times when she is not in the mood. For her part, the wife should realize how the prejudices she learnt from her parents are influencing her behaviour: and that prejudices can be unlearnt. They both must try their best to make the sexual side of their marriage enriching for the whole relationship. This communion of bodies and minds should help them to come closer to each other in a deepening knowledge of each other's needs and inclinations. Instead of dividing them, their sexuality should help to unite them as a couple and lead them to lasting happiness together. They must remember that they are a couple: both husband and wife can do what they like, with the one proviso that neither must do anything they know their partner does not like. What is important is unity: 'Let's get to the bottom of this problem together!'

The story has a happy ending. Our troubled couple came to regard their sexual activities as a shared activity, one in which they refused to take either their successes or their failures too seriously. After a few shaky beginnings, the sexual side of their marriage became a small but important part of their whole, loving relationship. They were able to talk about it freely and without shame or inhibitions, and were thus able to give each other confidence. Overcoming their problems together strengthened their unity as a couple, and ended the excessive emphasis on their sexual relationship that had resulted from their early failures.

7

CHILDREN AND CHILD-REARING

SOME PREREQUISITES

Parents and teachers alike seem to find it increasingly difficult to rear and educate children today. If we bring the subject of child-rearing and education into our book about peaceful partnerships, it is because this important subject gives rise to a great deal of dissension between partners, and also because everyone in the family, parents and children alike, must play a part in maintaining a friendly, peaceful atmosphere in the home. Rudolf Dreikurs and I dealt with this matter more fully in our book on parents and children.[18]

All the major religions emphasize that parents should educate their children to be believers. If children do not have the benefit of religious guidance, or at least have some moral values instilled into them, they will resort to working out such things for themselves, not always satisfactorily. For the most part they lose their sense of direction and find it difficult to accept authority. This may be expressed in lack of respect for their parents, which, taken to its logical conclusion, can be interpreted as a refusal to obey God. Such children tend, therefore, to lack proper consideration for other people and to be preoccupied with their own concerns. Ultimately, they are motivated entirely by the pleasure principle. This does not bode well for their future partnerships.

Modern psychology has, however, perfected new, effective methods of child education consistent with the teachings of the major religions, which all parents, regardless of their level of education or training, can use as guiding principles in the education of their children. They originate mainly from Adlerian psychology, particularly the work of Alfred Adler and one of his most eminent pupils, Rudolf Dreikurs, which, of all the different schools of psychology, has paid most attention to educational matters.

As a prerequisite for effective child education, parents today must make every effort to understand their children, whose attitudes and feelings are quite different from their own, even at the same age. Formerly, society was totally supportive of parents and parental authority: 'Children should be seen but not heard'. Today, however, social equality is the aim for everyone, regardless of age or sex, and today's children expect to be treated as individuals with their own rights.

Parents, if they wish to understand a child, must also take account of the circumstances and culture in which that child is growing up. Considerable changes have come about in the space of just one generation. But if parents want to establish a real rapport with their children and educate them effectively, they must also understand themselves and the reasons for their actions, expectations and goals, which are often subconscious. The new psychological methods, many of which we have discussed in this book, are particularly relevant here, because they enable parents to learn a great deal about themselves.

Finally, an understanding of the position that the major religions take on education is important because religion is like a rock of established laws and principles amid the shifting currents of popular trends. Education, therefore, should take account of moral and religious teaching as well as academic matters. 'Abdu'l-Bahá sums it up in his description of a father's duty to his child:

'He must give him advice and exhort him at all times, teach him praiseworthy conduct and character, enable him to receive training at school and to be instructed in such arts and sciences as are deemed useful and necessary. In brief, let him instil into his mind the virtues and perfections of the world of humanity. Above all he should continually call to his mind the remembrance of God.'[19]

THE MAIN PRINCIPLES

Here, then, are the four principles of child-rearing. The first is order. I am not talking merely about tidiness, but the need to subject our thoughts, our feelings, our beliefs and our behaviour to an over-riding order and coherence. Here a decisive role is played by the atmosphere within the family, the parents' own example, and the way family members respect each other's rights and fulfil their responsibilities. Religion can also play a very significant part in achieving order and consistency in all areas of our lives. Having achieved order in our own homes, we can work for order in the world and happiness and peace for all its people.

The second principle is to avoid letting disagreements and clashes of opinions escalate into aggressive conflict in the form of full-blown quarrels. Parents can quickly get to know which types of discussion tend to lead to arguments or disagreements. One thing should be obvious to us all: we cannot educate through arguments, nor can either parent or child win. Parents should also make a point of never getting mixed up in children's quarrels, but should keep their distance and choose the most fruitful way of intervening. The less frequently parents intervene, the more meaningful their interventions will be: we should therefore stay on the sidelines until there is something useful we can say or do. Of course, we should always intervene to prevent an exchange of blows. When small children squabble, parents can easily create a diversion or even tell a funny story to distract the children's attention, but all children can be trained to be more restrained with one another or, as a last resort, to leave the room before an argument erupts. Above all, parents must set a good example to show that worthwhile people do not resort to conflict or violence. We must teach our children that peace at home is the first step towards peace on earth.

The third principle, which is esteemed as a fundamental virtue by all the major religions, is encouragement. You can only give courage to a child if you have faith in him. Never despair of him, but love and trust him – not as you would like him to be, but just as he is, with a full and clear understanding of all his faults and weaknesses. To be accepted for ourselves is the most encouraging thing of all, because it proves that despite all our shortcomings someone believes in the good within us. Although parents will find it impossible to approve of every aspect of a child's behaviour, they can still praise the efforts he makes and applaud his small everyday achievements. In order to be encouraging, parents should adopt a positive attitude. They should listen as attentively to a child's feelings and views as they would to a friend's conversation. They must never be ashamed of letting the child see their own mistakes and weaknesses, nor of asking his help from time to time, just as he can count on theirs. This will not undermine their authority: rather, it will strengthen the parent–child relationship.

The final principle is the fear of God. Parents who are not themselves believers should at least try to develop a philosophy of life for themselves, together with the moral precepts this involves. Children need a firm set of values, something they can steer a course by and against which they can judge their own actions; even something to rebel against from time to time. Left to themselves children will develop their own values, but they may not be very worthwhile ones, and may not satisfy our first principle, that of order and consistency.

'Fear of God' is an expression that will surprise and even shock some people, as today it is regarded as a rather old-fashioned concept. It has, however, nothing to do with being *afraid* of God. A God-fearing person is one who tries to live his life in obedience to His commandments for love of God; and those commandments are nothing more nor less than rules that enable us to live better and more fully. In primitive times, fear of God was often confused with fear of God's anger. Today it is more often regarded as a loving call from God's love to the love that is within us, asking us to live our lives according to His laws. If we choose, it can be a standard for our life, to which it gives meaning; and now more than ever our children need this kind of support, because in today's society standards and meaning are hard to find. As it is waritten in the Old Testament, 'The fear of the Lord is the beginning of wisdom.'[20]

Zarathustra tells how the soul of every righteous person is met by a beautiful maiden. 'I am your fear of God,' she says. 'I am your good thoughts, words and deeds.' She takes his hand and leads him across a bridge that represents all he has made of these things during his time on earth, towards the eternal light. Finally, fear of God releases us from earthly fears: Friedrich Rueckert said: 'Son, fear God, so that your heart may be without fear; for the fear of God will set you free from the fears of men.'

THE MAIN METHODS

Although it is possible to attach too much importance to parental influences, we must not disregard them either, especially when we consider the vital role of encouragement. It is natural for all young creatures to look up to their parents and learn from them. Like baby animals, children copy their parents' behaviour, especially negative behaviour!

However, they do not merely imitate. The human child has an inventive faculty all his own, which enables him to make independent decisions – sometimes doing the exact opposite of whatever is expected of him. For example, a child from a criminal family very often ends up with a criminal record himself, but he may also decide that he does not want to grow up like his father, and can instead look around for other examples to follow. Parents are therefore not necessarily to blame for their children's misdeeds, nor can they take all the credit for their achievements; it is no easy task to unravel the tangled skein of influences and responses that make us what we are at any given moment. However, there are certain methods of child-rearing that will help us to be better parents.

Observation

Observation of the child and her behaviour should be at the top of our list. This alone will put us on our guard against acting on impulse. Experienced educators avoid snap reactions because they would then be giving up control to the child: she has misbehaved in the hope of provoking such a reaction, and now she has the upper hand. The adults find themselves playing the child's game, by her rules, and thereby doing exactly as she expects and wishes. However well we parents think we know our children, we do not know them nearly as well as they know us!

Through observation we get to know the child and the things that influence her: the age she lives in, her environment, most of all her brothers and sisters. Siblings generally exert a greater influence on her life than her parents do. It is therefore very helpful to understand how children behave according to their position in the family group, or what Adler called the 'family constellation'.

The first child, while he remains an only child, feels monarch of all he surveys until he is dethroned by the arrival of a second child. There is usually rivalry, therefore, between the first two children. When one is good, the other is bad; when one excels at something, the other feels unable to compete. The younger child always feels dominated by his older, stronger and more advanced sibling. He can react either by struggling to catch up, and if possible overtake, his older brother or, depending on their differences in age and sex, by accepting a subordinate role and looking to him for support and protection. They will remain competitors, but are no longer intense rivals. In extreme cases, if the elder child is particularly gifted or outstanding, the younger child can feel profoundly discouraged. He gives up the struggle and looks for some other route to superiority.

The third child observes her older siblings and frequently chooses one of two alternatives. Either she refuses to take part in the competition and develops an irresistible charm that gains her recognition without much effort, or she may, especially if she is the youngest child in the family, resolve to catch up with her older siblings and even outstrip them. Of course, these decisions are largely made at the subconscious level, rather than consciously. It is also important to understand that a child is influenced primarily by her own interpretation of her circumstances rather than by the circumstances alone. Different children invariably react in different ways to the same situation, and develop their own personal strategies in their family relationships. Readers wishing to explore the effect of family constellations on themselves, their partners or their children will find a more detailed discussion in my earlier book, *The Way to Inner Freedom*.[21]

This kind of analysis shows how indispensable it is to observe children, especially when they are playing or otherwise interacting. The insight thus gained enables parents to intervene at the right time and correct developments which, if ignored, could harm the child's spiritual growth.

Consideration

The second main method is consideration. After observing our child we need to take some time to think carefully about what we have observed, which will help us to speak less. Speech is a means of transmitting messages and information but, contrary to popular belief, it is not an educational tool in itself. Unfortunately, so many parents are used to speaking *to* their children, and have not yet learnt the art of talking *with* them. They think that they can educate with words, words that consist of eternally making rules and regulations for their children. However, no one likes to be controlled by other people – not even children – and constantly being told what to do merely sensitizes them to advice, perhaps for the rest of their lives! Consequently, taking the time to think carefully before responding to our child will discourage us from over-hasty reactions that only poison the atmosphere.

The most important question to consider while observing our child's behaviour is which of the five unconscious short-term goals the child is pursuing, and why. (To refresh your memory about these goals, see Chapter 3.) Having got to the root of the problem, we are in a better position to deal with it effectively, or at least to recognize what we should not do in a given situation. Careful consideration of our child's actions and trying to understand her will also help us to dismiss the prejudices and confusing misconceptions that are current in both psychology and in society today. These include the over-emphasis of issues like heredity, predisposition, drives, facts, lack of will-power, lack of concentration, sensitivity, immaturity and so on. The truly decisive issue we must consider is how much courage and concern for others – what Adler termed 'social interest' – our child has, and how we can help him or her to develop these qualities.

Developing the right attitude

The third main method to apply to child education is for parents to have the right attitude to their child and his situation. If we are already putting into practice in our families the four principles we discussed earlier – order, avoiding arguments, encouragement and the fear of God – we will find ourselves becoming increasingly more aware and more spiritual as individuals and, of course, as parents. Almost every example of bad behaviour in a child can be traced back to one or other of these principles being neglected. This only serves to emphasize how important it is to develop the right attitude to parenting and to our children.

By right attitude I mean that positive approach to the task of parenting that implies acceptance of difficulties, a willingness to tackle problems, and the optimism and confidence to act constructively. Running away from family difficulties or trying to ignore them can only aggravate the initial problem and further discourage us, forcing us to make excuses for ourselves. Consequently, as we noted at the beginning of the last chapter, we should not expect perfection, or to be able to solve all our parenting problems and get instant results from our efforts. We should rather have faith in ourselves and in our children, and welcome problems as challenges we can rise to meet, and learn something from in the process.

However, achieving a positive attitude as parents is more difficult if we have not put enough effort into achieving it in our partnership. Children are profoundly affected by their home environment and any discord between parents is immediately picked up and reflected in their behaviour. Above all we should realize that the basis of a happy family is the spiritual union of the couple.

In correcting children's misbehaviour it is important to remember the point we mentioned earlier: to hate the sin and love the sinner – and to make this clear to the child. This has an incredibly positive and encouraging effect on her. When a child does something naughty, her father and mother usually react by showing their displeasure – or worse. The child then feels rejected and unloved. But a child whose parents show that they still love her whatever mischief she has been up to, but they do not accept her behaviour, will react quite differently. She can then confront her misdeeds without the weight of guilt and anxiety which, far from helping her to behave better in future, only leads to further misbehaviour. Thus when parents distinguish between the deed and the doer, the child will not doubt her parents' love and will try to behave better next time.

One further element of the positive approach in childrearing is to aim for firmness and friendliness. We need to be friendly towards our children, but also quite firm about what we think is right and what, consequently, we will and will not accept. Generally speaking our children are just as intelligent as us, their parents, and will continually test us to the limit, trying to see just how far they can go.

Action

Finally, a word about action, the last method we need to discuss. This does not necessarily mean punishing misbehaviour, but rather taking action to make sure it does not happen again. Acting in the right way is a far better method of educating children than any amount of 'lecturing', and stops us being authoritarian: we should try to be both friendly *and* firm at the same time, neither argue nor give in, make time for the child, experience pleasure together, and develop a fairly settled daily routine. Moreover, we must always try to act immediately, with the goal not of punishing the child but of giving him greater responsibility – and as early as possible. Punishment as such is out of favour today. Many people have found it is better to let the child suffer the natural consequences of his misbehaviour. Repeatedly saying, 'If you don't hurry up you'll be late for school' is far less effective than allowing the child to miss the school bus – once is usually enough. This is just as unpleasant for the child as any so-called punishment.

Letting nature take its course, rather than imposing some authoritarian rule, has the advantage of making the child take responsibility for his own actions and showing him that he is regarded as a person in his own right. Moreover, behind the punishment stands the authority of a single person like the father or mother, which the modern child in our age of equality can no longer recognize, while behind the consequences stands the authority of the group, for example the family, which children find more acceptable. Thus a child who is only too ready to rebel against parental authority soon realizes how stupid and pointless it is to rebel against the natural and logical consequences of his own actions.

Most modern parents agree that smacking is no way to treat, let alone educate, a child. Even so, there is still far too much punishment going on – heaping abuse on him, sending him to his room, no TV, no outings, no pudding, no pocket money, and so on. Children do not respect such strictures, but rather resent them as just another example of the rough justice meted out by authoritarian adults.

The old adage of 'prevention is better than cure' applies especially to child-rearing. It is much more effective to keep a careful eye on the child and, at the first sign of an undesirable character trait, gently counsel the child in a loving, friendly way. The younger the child, the more successful the preventive approach can be, while nipping problems 'in the bud' – which requires our observation and consideration – helps avoid the necessity for harsher measures such as reprimands and punishments.

Another effective way of acting is to show the child his short-term goals. The aim is to encourage the child to review his behaviour and to understand better his reasons for misbehaving. However, it is very important that this is done in the right way – in a positive and loving spirit, with no trace of criticism or superiority, which would only serve to offend or put down the child. This subject is dealt with in greater depth in the book on parenting I co-authored with Rudolf Dreikurs.[18] Finally, one of the most effective ways of acting is the introduction of a family council.

The family council

Every time something happens that affects the whole family, it is an excellent idea to get into the habit of bringing the whole family together to discuss it. It could be anything from holiday plans, choice of school, moving house or a sudden change in the family fortunes, to health problems, sibling disputes or anxieties about a friend or relation. There is no need to be too formal: the subject can be brought up over a meal and a time arranged for discussing the matter together.

Many readers may be surprised that I say the whole family should take part. Past generations did not pay much heed to children and even forbade them to speak, but when they are given the opportunity, children can make a worthwhile contribution to family discussions at a surprisingly early age. Therefore, as soon as a child is able to speak, she should be encouraged to take part.

Basically, a family council is a forum for collective decision-making and problem-solving, and therefore really needs a chairperson. This does not require an officious, domineering manner, of course, but simply entails being responsible for maintaining order in the meeting, encouraging each person to participate in the consultation, making sure everyone gets a chance to voice their opinions, and gently restraining others who try to talk too much. The parents do not need to chair the meeting – in fact ideally the chair rotates, as does the duty of taking minutes. With help, even a child can learn very early on how to chair the meeting and how to take notes. Not all families will want to go so far as to have minutes, but it is worth pointing out the benefit of keeping a note of all resolutions: unanimous agreement is not always possible, and experience tells us that those who 'lost out' in the vote will have a bad memory when it comes to recalling the decision!

The advantages and pitfalls

'Family consultation, employing full and frank discussion animated by awareness of the need for moderation and balance, can be the panacea for domestic conflict.'[22]

A family in the habit of holding get-togethers of this kind benefits considerably. The family council shifts the authority for making decisions from the 'head' of the family – usually the father – to the whole group, for the common good. If the family has older children, of fifteen or more, then the family council is virtually a necessity. It is almost impossible for an individual parent to influence older children, especially if they are discouraged and lack confidence in themselves. However, these children find it easier to recognize the authority of the whole family group –

116

and accept its advice. Here lies the primary value of the council – it carries the responsibility for everything that happens in the family that affects more than one family member. This follows the logic that two heads are better than one, and enables everyone to learn that decisions are a matter of participation, not compliance with the whim of just one person.

Many parents find it difficult to give up what they regard as their responsibility to the group, but once they see the benefits for the children and the family as a unit, they will welcome the council. For children, it represents a positive opportunity to participate in the family on a new level and learn valuable lessons, which can be very encouraging. They also learn that it is not wrong to express their own opinion, and that through sharing our different viewpoints, a better decision can usually be reached. As 'Abdu'l-Bahá observed: 'The shining spark of truth cometh forth only after the clash of differing opinions.'[23]

By involving every member of the family in the decision-making process, family councils – if conducted correctly – teach everyone how to think and how to take sensible decisions, even if these decisions go against their own inclinations. Children learn to speak out freely and clearly, to say what is on their minds and, above all, to listen carefully. A family in which everyone has a right to self-expression and a duty to listen to others, where everyone can speak frankly, is a splendid training ground for life.

The family is a living cell in which the child gains his first experience of living with and for other people in peace. There his eccentricities are accepted, and he learns to accept the eccentricities of others. The family council provides an unrivalled opportunity for family members to gain a deeper understanding of each other and themselves, and to develop their social skills. True social maturity depends on qualities like tolerance, fairness, detachment, generosity, lack of prejudice, social interest and courage, qualities that are fostered in the consultation process of family councils.

So far I have outlined only the advantages of the council. There are also pitfalls to avoid, and the council must be conducted properly if we are to avoid these. When a question of relationships or of conduct arises within the family, the family council will discuss it just as naturally as any other matter. But care must of course be taken, especially by the chairperson, to make sure the consultation does not degenerate into a court of inquiry. The family council has no right to judge any of its members, far less to condemn them. It has the right only to seek the best means of solving a problem as harmoniously as possible and to offer a helping hand to anyone who needs it. Let me repeat just once more: there is no such thing as a difficult person; there is only difficult behaviour.

Like every discussion, family consultation can also run the risk of degenerating into long-winded debate with no decision-making power whatsoever. It is important not to value fine words at the expense of sound judgement. Family councils should be serious, but never solemn or pompous. Laughter is encouraged, but not at other people's expense, especially that of younger or less experienced people trying to contribute to the discussion. All members of the family must learn to keep the purpose of the consultation firmly in mind and to exercise courtesy and moderation in the expression of their views. Otherwise they risk seeing their loving consultation more closely resemble a verbal punch-up or an ego trip. It also goes without saying that a family council is not the place to pursue private power struggles between individual members of the family. In such a competitive environment, feelings are liable to be hurt, and instead of being an enriching, unifying occasion where everyone works together, the meeting will simply stir the embers of discord – and discouragement and disunity will result.

We must always bear in mind when we consult together the factors that cause conflict (discussed in Chapter 5) and try to put into practice our five basic rules of conflict-solving (Chapter 6). Consultation is in reality an art, and if we try to develop our consultation skills, and our motives are pure, we can go a long way to avoiding most of the pitfalls we have discussed. The family council may start off slowly and awkwardly, and the parents will have to show the way – but what wonderful training for everyone!

8

A FINAL WORD

SEPARATION AND DIVORCE

At the beginning of this book, I mentioned the increase
in the divorce rate in the twentieth century, and the simul-
taneous and more or less world-wide drop in the number
of marriages. Couples who are unhappy together can
indeed divorce or separate, but at the cost of breaking up
the marriage without solving their underlying problems.
Both separation and divorce leave everyone involved feeling – consciously or otherwise – a failure. Then both ex-
partners try hard to salve their uneasy consciences by
blaming the failure of their marriage on each other. There
are, no doubt, some cases where the blame lies entirely
on one side; but not many. There is usually wrong on
both sides: both partners have made mistakes. Moreover,
divorce and separation do not help anyone. On the contrary, they can scar people for life, leaving them dreadfully
hurt and discouraged.

   If the couple have had a family, it is usually the children
who suffer most. Their future, their development, their
temperament and their entire happiness are affected,
sometimes irrevocably. This is particularly true when their

parents use them as pawns in their ongoing battle, or fight over them as if they were 'possessions'. Divorcing couples should never forget that, whatever their legal status, they are still a couple by reason of their children, for children cannot divorce their parents. It is therefore wicked to subject children to the backwash of their parents' disputes and even worse if, as happens far too often, their parents ask them to take sides. Each parent must scrupulously avoid saying or doing anything that might damage the other parent's standing in the eyes of a child, for to do so would amount to making the child hate and condemn half of himself. Each parent must also guard against the temptation to spoil children in the hope of gaining their favours at the other parent's expense. All such goings-on injure children very deeply. So many innocent victims have suffered in this way, their whole lives marred by the results of what thoughtless parents dared to call their 'love'!

It is true that in certain cases, such as after years of violent argument and fighting, children might see their parents' separation as a release from intolerable strain. However, separation is never more than a poor second best for them. This is the case even where the couple have managed to split up relatively painlessly, and maintain reasonably amicable relations with their divorced partners. While this of course enables the children to come out of the experience with the minimum of damage, such a solution can never serve the children's interests as well as a united, happy family.

It is definitely wise for the law to insist on a period of separation before granting a divorce. This gives both partners time to think about the tremendous step they are taking, and it can be something of a blessing provided that this period is not used simply to find a replacement for the partner, but for some serious soul-searching and self-analysis. Only when we truly come to know our own character and motives can we judge both ourselves and our partners more justly. If we are willing to forget the past as soon as we have learnt from it and begun to understand the real problems that lay beneath the surface, we will be able to see many things in a clearer and more objective light. All that is needed is courage: courage to let bygones be bygones, to be positive, to share responsibility, to have faith in ourselves, our partners and our relationship, and to turn resolutely to the future. When both partners are ready to put the past behind them instead of constantly finding fault with themselves or each other, a shared new beginning can have an excellent chance of succeeding.

This is why a woman who came to a psychotherapist for counselling about her impending separation was told, 'A divorce is the best solution. But before that, you really need to sort out your marriage!' It sounded a strange piece of advice, but the woman understood what the doctor meant. She examined her past behaviour, resolved to do better and made every effort to believe in and encourage both herself and her husband. The change in her behaviour affected her husband's attitude, their relationship improved, and divorce was no longer discussed, for the two partners had learnt to live peacefully together. Sadly, not all cases have such a satisfactory outcome, which takes an effort from both partners.

If a couple have not learnt to have frank and open discussions and to talk out their problems together, it can be beneficial to ask friends, counsellors or therapists to help them to do this. A book like this one can also be helpful, especially if both partners are prepared to read and learn from it. If, in spite of everything, divorce is unavoidable, it is important for both partners, before embarking on a new relationship, to seek specialist counselling to help them avoid making the same old mistakes with a new partner.

The objective of this book is to show that unity, and therefore peace, can be created in marriage, and to increase the chances of this happening. It is meant to help the reader to avoid separation and divorce if at all possible, since they are deeply discouraging to those involved, and do not bring us happiness, even though they may give us a momentary feeling of freedom. Couples should try their best to spare themselves and their children this trauma. It is obvious, however, that as long as our society encourages people to ignore the ordered, spiritual side of life and to abandon themselves to their unconscious impulses, divorce will be seen as the only way out. Not many people are willing to admit that they are not in control of their lives, but rather are at the mercy of superficial influences and their own emotions. As Alfred Adler observed, all individuals are decision-making human beings, responsible for their own feelings and behaviour – and capable of changing them. I have tried to show here that it is within everyone's power to become more conscious, more self-determined, and to achieve greater peace with their partners as a result.

EVERYONE CAN LEARN

Finally, let me set out my message once more. Every individual can learn:

to believe that people can change
to accept the social equality of man and woman
to make decisions consciously and responsibly

123

to recognize the power of belief
to allow themselves to be led by the word of God
to have a positive attitude to life
to choose a direction for their lives, and follow it
to choose a partner more consciously
to stop wanting to be right all the time
to recognize the importance of discussion
to become less emotional and more loving
to act, rather than simply react
to become less self-centred and more spiritual
to believe more in themselves and in their partners
. . . and to believe in lasting happiness rather than fleet-
ing moments of pleasure.

NOTES

1. The Universal House of Justice, *The Promise of World Peace*, pp. 28–32. Oneworld Publications, 1986.
2. *New English Bible*, Matthew VI: 25–34.
3. 'Abdu'l-Bahá, *Paris Talks*, p. 143. UK Bahá'í Publishing Trust, 1979.
4. Bahá'u'lláh, *Tablets of Bahá'u'lláh*, p. 173. Bahá'í World Centre, 1978.
5. 'Abdu'l-Bahá, quoted in *Bahá'u'lláh and the New Era*, p. 88. UK Bahá'í Publishing Trust, 1974.
6. See Alfred Adler, *What Life Could Mean To You*, pp. 16–19. Oneworld Publications, 1991.
7. Shoghi Effendi, quoted in *Principles of Bahá'í Administration*, pp. 12–13. UK Bahá'í Publishing Trust, 1976.
8. Emerson, *Journals*, 1854.
9. *New English Bible*, I Corinthians XIII: 7.
10. Bahá'u'lláh, *The Four Valleys*, p. 58. US Bahá'í Publishing Trust, 1978.
11. Shoghi Effendi, from a letter written on his behalf to an individual, 15 May, 1944.
12. Rudyard Kipling, *If*.
13. Max Planck, quoted in Sterneder, *Das Kosmische Weltbild*.
14. Bahá'u'lláh, *The Hidden Words*, p. 52. Oneworld Publications, 1986.
15. *King James Bible*, John VIII: 7.

16. Johann Wolfgang von Goethe, *Faust: Part I*.
17. Alexander Pope, *An Essay on Criticism*, line 525.
18. Rudolf Dreikurs & Erik Blumenthal, *Eltern und Kinder – Freunde oder Feinde?* Ernst-Klatt Verlag, 1973.
19. 'Abdu'l-Bahá, quoted in *Family Life*, pp. 9–10. UK Bahá'í Publishing Trust, 1982.
20. *King James Bible*, Psalms 111:10.
21. Erik Blumenthal, *The Way to Inner Freedom*, pp. 72–9. Oneworld Publications, 1988. See also Alfred Adler, *Understanding Human Nature*, pp. 126–32. Oneworld Publications, 1991.
22. The Universal House of Justice, 1 August 1978, quoted in *Family Life*, p. 30.
23. 'Abdu'l-Bahá, *Selections from the Writings of 'Abdu'l-Bahá*, p. 87. Bahá'í World Centre, 1978.